ATTENTION TO DETAIL

A Step by Step Guide on How to Make a Six-Figure Income Cleaning Houses

TIM ROSSHIRT

Tim Rosshirt

Printed in the United States of America

First Printing: 09/2024

Printed by: Amazon KDP

ISBN 97983391998475

ATTENTION TO DETAIL

A Step by Step Guide on How to Make a Six-Figure Income Cleaning Houses

de-tail (according to Webster's Dictionary): extended treatment of or attention to particular items

ABOUT TIM ROSSHIRT

Tim Rosshirt started General Cleaning Service with his first client, an uncle, in 1986, and closed the business when he said good-bye to his final client, Lou Ann, in 2018.

During his 32 years in business, Tim paid Attention to Detail for those on a strong client list that included a lawyer for whom a major law school was named in his memory, the president of a Big 10 university in the Midwest, the director of a large metropolitan transit system, a renowned pediatric surgeon at a well-known children's hospital, the CEO of a national fast-food burger chain, the founder of a national motel chain, a city council president, the founder and president of a major international corporation, and many other notables. Over the years, Tim was featured in major news publications.

In 2006, Tim made his first humanitarian trip to Zimbabwe, Africa to bring food and aid to impoverished villages. In 2009, he founded the Rosshirt Water for Africa Foundation which to date has raised funds to build and maintain 13 wells (boreholes). These wells continue to provide safe water to more than 80,000 people in rural and desolate regions of Zimbabwe every day. Visit the foundation website online at https://www.rosshirtwaterforafricafoundation.com/ to learn more.

Attention to Detail is in honor of my mother, Mary Rosshirt, who taught me how to clean and have an amazing work ethic. It is also dedicated to Alpha Mansaray – for his inspiration and help.

PREFACE

You'll find throughout this book quotes and passages that serve as guiding principles to me in my everyday life. I have discovered that these principles have greatly aided in the success of my career and personal life. I hope they will do the same for you.

INTRODUCTION

Attention to Detail is the story of my life, covering more than 32 years as a professional house cleaner and small business owner. This all started when I was just 23 years old and was a rewarding time for me personally and financially. I was in demand to clean luxury homes in Ohio and many clients' out-of-state vacation homes. Business was good, and grew to the point where eventually I was earning a significant six-figure income every year. However, I would not have done so well if I did not **give top-notch, detailed service** from the start to people who expect nothing but the best in every area of their lives.

In June 2018, I closed my business, General Cleaning Service, to start a new phase of life and follow new passions. My first one was to write this book and help other dreamers follow their desire to start a successful cleaning business.

Are you that person? Do you have that burning desire? Do you have that dream? If so, this book is for you!

Even more, my book will teach you how to clean with such precision and professionalism that you'll attract all the clients you can handle, earn their respect, and keep them satisfied for years to come.

The cleaning system in Attention to Detail works for any setting, including:

- Homes from 1,000 to 100,000 square feet
- Five-star luxury hotels or national hotel chains
- Office buildings and corporate headquarters
- Assisted living facilities and nursing care centers

And more!

This book can also be a great resource for hotel managers, their executive housekeepers and cleaning staff; the owner of a beach-side bed and breakfast, or companies that manage vacation home/condo rentals. It is an easy-to-follow guide on how to provide white-glove, detailed and sanitary cleaning from top to bottom in any setting.

Finally, it will help those who already have a cleaning business and want to take it to the highest possible level.

In order to succeed, though, you **must have that high desire** to be the best cleaner in the area and have a strong drive to achieve professional success. *Attention to Detail* can take you to a level of success others only dream about – if you follow the step-by-step processes contained within each chapter.

Something Good is About to Happen!

TABLE OF CONTENTS

CHAPTER 1

MY STORY

I was born into a strong Catholic family and was one of nine children. Even before I was legally old enough to have a job, I worked because I knew that money could buy the things I wanted – the extra things that my parents couldn't afford. So I did what any hard-working boy did: I shoveled snow, raked leaves, and cut grass for the neighbors. I built a nice little business for myself because the neighbors liked the work I did.

Back then, I was already a perfectionist and everything had to be just right! Attention to detail was already part of my personality; when I was shoveling snow, the driveway and sidewalk edges had to be perfectly straight, and ALL the snow had to be removed. When I raked leaves, you can be sure there were no leaves left anywhere on the ground. In fact, I was picky enough that if any leaves fell on the ground after I finished raking, I went back and picked them up by hand.

As you can imagine, with a family of 11, there was "stuff" everywhere in my house, and that went against my need to have everything in perfect order. So, my first experience cleaning was in my own house, which I started taking care of after my mom began to work outside the home. She never asked me to, I just wanted to. I needed order in my life, and cleaning helped me create that order.

Not only was my bedroom perfect, the entire house and yard was clean and tidy – and I know that pleased my mother and made her life easier. I can honestly say that my compulsive need to clean when I was still a young teenager is what helped me to be successful for over 30 years. I can also say that, in my case, having an obsessive compulsive personality contributed to that success.

Driven by Money

I don't deny it, I love to make money! Money pays my bills, and money helps me have nice things. I love to work and I am a go-getter – and no matter what I do, I always give it my best. When I was younger and doing yard work for the neighbors, I thought it was just luck that I had so many customers. I realized later that it was my need to do it perfectly and my constant attention to detail that brought me as much business as I could handle.

As a child, my dream was to be the first in my family to graduate college and make lots of money. I never graduated college, but I did succeed in earning a six-figure income when I was still young. I started college, thinking I would study business, but stayed for only one semester. I dreaded starting the second semester because I felt trapped, and rather than going to my class that first day, I went to the admission's office and withdrew. I didn't look back, and I never had regrets - but I didn't have a plan, either.

While some people told me I'd made a big mistake, I knew that wasn't true. I applied for and got my first "real" job at a national auto parts retailer. Even then, my obsessive personality worked for me because I wanted the job and I wanted it now! I hounded the human resources department every day for several days until they finally hired me. This was a courier job where I delivered car parts to gas stations, automotive service centers, etc. I also had to pick up and bring back old batteries, brakes, rotors and other dirty used car parts. This was not in my comfort zone because I didn't like getting dirty, and this was definitely a dirty job. Even so, my need for perfection kicked in and I stayed perfectly clean every day, which I thought was a good thing. What it actually did was make me stand out as the oddball in a business where dirty is normal. It didn't take long before I realized that I didn't like the job, but I still went to work every day and did my best.

I needed to take control of my life and destiny, and knew I had to figure out my plan. The little voices inside my head were asking questions I had no immediate answer for. Questions like: "What are you going to do with the rest of your life? What job will make you happy and bring in a lot of money? What can you do really well?"

Suddenly one day, I just knew. Cleaning – that's what I did best. So in 1986, at just 23 years old, I started to plan my cleaning business. I told my family about these plans at a holiday get-together, and my uncle said he would be my first customer. I had a client! I cleaned his house once a week. Then out of the blue, a former teacher who knew I was looking to start a cleaning business suggested that I call the administrator at our local school district. She knew they were looking for someone to clean one of the buildings and thought I would be a good person for the job.

I went to the interview with confidence in my abilities, looking and sounding like someone who had been in business for years. I got the job on the spot.

Lesson Learned: *Talk about your business every chance you get.*

My next client was someone I'd known for a while, Ronda, who rented space in a local salon to do nails. We ran into each other one day and began talking, and I told her about my new cleaning business. Coincidentally, she needed someone to clean her space. I gave her an estimate for cleaning and as they say, the rest is history. I cleaned her workspace for the first time that same week, and did more than clean and get rid of nail dust. I knew that I was taking a chance, but even so, I moved her work station and furnishings around to make that space more open and functional. Ronda loved it – and so would be her clients!

Going the extra mile and doing more than Ronda expected was a smart move on my part. In less than two months, I went from 2 clients to 10 simply because Ronda told her clients about the amazing cleaner she had and many wanted to have me clean their homes. In turn, my new clients told their friends about this great cleaner they had. Over the following years, my business continued to grow, and as I became more in demand, I was able to raise my hourly rate.

I am proud that for over 30 years, I was valued by my clients because I paid **attention to detail and I was 100% honest!**

Lesson Learned: *The things that come most quickly into your life are the things that you BELIEVE in the most.*

-The Secret Daily Teachings

It didn't take long to realize that the reason I was getting – and keeping – clients was because I did more than just clean better than others. I paid attention to every detail and gave each client more value for their money. Their homes were in perfect order when I left, and that's what they wanted and expected. I can honestly say that I was more particular than most of my clients – which made them happy!

Anticipate, anticipate and anticipate some more!

I always tried to anticipate a need before a client asked, and I never wanted a client to tell me I missed something. To me, that meant I wasn't doing do my job. I would always look around the home to see if something needed a little more attention; for instance, the carpets or windows needed to be cleaned. I had a list of preferred contractors that I knew did the job right, and that were reliable and trustworthy – and clients always appreciated that. They knew that if the contractor lived up to my high standards, the work would be done perfectly.

I also provided extra services, like cleaning and organizing closets, even though that wasn't what I was expected to do. A couple of times, a client called to say he or she was coming home sick when I was at the home cleaning. I made sure the bedroom was done first, with the bed turned down and ready to climb into. There were also times when a client seemed particularly rushed in the morning and I offered to take the children to school. These touches are little things that don't take a whole lot of effort, but definitely make a difference to the clients.

From the time I took on my first job cutting grass to saying thank you and good-bye to my last cleaning client in June 2018, there were three constants in my professional relationships:

- I was honest.

- I took extreme pride in my work.

- I took care of each home as if it were my own.

Part of this is due to the values my parents instilled in myself and my siblings, and much of this is due to my compulsion for perfection, attention to detail, and inner drive to always succeed.

Lesson Learned: *Be a ray of sunshine to everyone you meet, and make their day better for having seen you.*

The Secret Daily Teachings

Last, I recommend using the four agreements below to help to guide your actions.

The Four Agreements

- *Be impeccable with your word: Speak with integrity. Say only what you mean. Avoid using the word to speak against yourself or to gossip about others. Use the power of your word in the direction of truth and love.*

- *Don't take anything personally: Nothing others do is because of you. What others say and do is a projection of their own reality. When you are immune to the opinions and actions of others, you won't be the victim of needless suffering.*

- *Don't make assumptions: Find the courage to ask questions and to express what you really want. Communicate with others as clearly as you can to avoid misunderstandings, sadness, and drama. With just this one agreement, you can completely transform your life.*

- *Always do your best: Your best is going to change from moment to moment; it will be different when you are healthy as opposed to sick. Under any circumstance, simply do your best, and you will avoid self-judgment, self-abuse, and regret.*

- Don Miguel Ruiz

CHAPTER 2

FINDING CLIENTS

Y ou took that first big step and decided to start your cleaning business. Congratulations! Now you need to continue the process and become one of the highest paid house cleaners in the city. You can make it happen by doing your best every day, constantly improving your cleaning and time management skills, and staying focused and determined.

Finding clients for your new business may seem challenging at first. Just know you can do it. After all, you have the passion, drive, and confidence in yourself and your ability. Wake up each morning and say, *I can and I will do this!*

Man is what he believes. — Anton Chekhov

Be Ready!

Before you start looking for clients, be 100% sure that you have completely mastered the cleaning process, including knowing how long each step or task will take. Do this by cleaning and re-cleaning your own home and even the home of a family member or friend to make sure you are at the level of detail and perfection that is stressed throughout this book.

Professional Executive Cleaning Service

Email: **email address.com**   Phone: **555-5555**

Estimate sheet prepared for

Date: ___________________

Name: ____   Phone: _______________

Street: ____

State: __________   Zip: _________________   Email: ________________________________

MAJOR CLEANING

Includes washing all woodwork in home; sweep and vacuum floors and under all furniture; wash every knick-knack in home by hand; detail kitchen and baths; change linens and make beds; take items out of the china cabinet, wash by hand and return(optional); clean oven, stove top and refrigerator inside and out; scrub floors and other details agreed upon.

Client Remarks: ____

____

Major Cleaning: $___________________________

WEEKLY (or other) CLEANING

Services include clean and wax furniture; clean and detail bathrooms; scrub floors on hands and knees; straighten accessories/wall hangings; clean pictures; clean outside kitchen cabinets; detail kitchen; make beds/change linens; spot clean walls and light controls; vacuum and dust entire home.

Client Remarks: ____

____

Frequency of Cleaning: ☐ Weekly   ☐ Bi-Weekly   ☐ Monthly

Weekly (or other) Cleaning: $___________________

Major Cleaning: $___________________

TOTAL: $___________________

Not included: Windows. Ask about fees for this and other services not listed.

You should also have professional business cards made and an Estimate Sheet ready to use. The example shown here is something you can easily make on the computer and includes the basic information you need to prepare an estimate. Also, at the end of this chapter is a list of *Frequently Asked Questions* – these are questions I found that potential clients generally asked me.

How to Get New Clients

When you are confident that you're ready for clients, start spreading the word through family, friends, and service providers you personally use, like a dry cleaner, hair stylist/barber, or your doctor or dentist. Don't be shy – tell anyone you think would let others know about your new cleaning business. Start talking to folks when you are shopping and waiting in line, mingling with others at church, or at your children's school – anyplace there are people. Keep business cards with you at all times.

Most of my new clients came through referrals from existing clients. One thing about client referrals is that the potential client most likely knows what your hourly cleaning rate is – and that is half the battle. Referrals are the best way to get new clients, but it does take time to get to the point where you have clients that are comfortable enough with your services to refer you to their friends and family.

Advertising for new clients is another option, but it can be expensive, and you need to be selective about where to advertise. I only advertised a few times in 32 years. These ads were designed specifically for successful business professionals and placed in a monthly Columbus magazine geared to high-level executives and company CEOs.

There were times when someone seemed interested in my services, but wasn't quite willing to make that commitment. If that happens to you, offer to clean a room in their home for free so they can see how you can make it shine!

What Should You Charge?

Figure out your expenses, including workers, and determine a fair hourly rate. Don't just pull a figure out of the air and say, "this will be my hourly rate."

Think about the cost of living in your area. It is going to be higher in New York City or San Francisco than in Pittsburgh or Cleveland. Do your research online and talk to other small service business owners and ask how they came up with a price range. You can and should charge more than other cleaners because your cleaning services are going to be far superior to theirs.

HomeAdvisor.com has a report that allows you to input your zip code and find the typical cost for house cleaning services in your area. You can expect that cities with a high cost of living are going to have higher hourly rates, but you'll have higher expenses there, too. You can get the report online at https://www.homeadvisor.com/cost/cleaning-services/ to see the rates and get additional useful information.

Keep in mind when setting an initial hourly rate that this will probably be your price for a while. You shouldn't start increasing rates until you are more established, have a good client base and are becoming known as the cleaner to have. Consider the following points when talking with clients and/or preparing your estimate:

- If you bill for regular cleanings by the hour, your estimate should reflect an accurate number of hours, and you are sure that you'll get the job done each time in that number of hours."

- Keep in mind that there can be unexpected additional cleaning time needed at the home. If you quote a flat rate for a regular cleaning, what happens if the client has a party or family get-together around the holidays and there is a lot more to clean your next time at the home? Be clear when you give your initial estimate and quote a flat rate that if this happens, you normally bill the additional time at your hourly rate, and make sure the client knows what that hourly rate is. If the client doesn't agree to pay for extra hours, you should also be sure they know that you and your team will leave when you've reached the maximum hours for that cleaning.

- For a major cleaning, quote a flat rate, and let the client know what will be cleaned for that price and how many total hours the cleaning would take. This number of total hours will include all the people you have working with you on this cleaning. Let the client know that if the cleaning takes less time, they will be charged less based on the hours you spent at the home. At the same time, if the cleaning is taking longer than expected (through no fault of your own), let the client know what's happening and why. Let them decide if you should do more or if they want you to stop when you've reached the time limit and dollar amount you quoted.

- If your state requires sales tax, consult with a tax professional to ensure you're correctly applying and collecting sales tax, and that you're following all applicable regulations. Ohio does have a sales tax; each county can have its own tax rate and it's important to do it right and avoid fines or penalties.

The Universe has unlimited ways to bring your dream about, and I can assure you that when you emanate your dream on the inside of you, it will appear in the outside world in a way that you could never have imagined. Just get your emanation happening and leave the rest to the Universe.

The Secret Daily Teachings

Give Accurate Quotes

The more new clients you get, the better you will become at giving realistic quotes. The following points can help guide you in figuring out the real cost of cleaning a client's home. Your clients won't want any surprises, especially if you have to tell them later that you underestimated the cost of cleaning their home. (It does happen though, so don't beat yourself up if you make a mistake!)

- Be clear and detailed about what will be cleaned in the client's home, and whether it's at an hourly or a flat rate.

- Give all estimates in written form – one copy to the client and another for your files.

- Let the client know that when there are guests or holiday events in the home, cleaning it will take longer and they will be invoiced for the extra time spent cleaning. Make sure your hourly rate for any extra hours is clearly listed in all estimates.

- Also be clear about what you expect from the client before you arrive at the home. For example, they have several children and you would like toys, clothing, shoes, backpacks – all the things that add clutter to a home and make it hard to clean around – put out of the way before you start cleaning. Explain that if they are unable to do this, you and your team will, but there will be an added cost.

Or perhaps there is a home office and the desk is always cluttered with papers. Make sure there is an understanding between you and the client. Do you lift papers up and clean beneath, then put them back, or simply ignore the desk and clean every other part of the room?

No matter the scenario, be sure they understand that if what you expect is not taken care of before you arrive to clean, they will be billed for the extra time it takes you and your team to finish the cleaning.

At some point, your hourly rate will increase. However, don't raise prices if you are still looking for more clients. You want to become the cleaner who is "in-demand" by potential clients before you start thinking about rate hikes for existing ones. All price increase announcements should be made in writing and not mailed, but given to each client in person. You should create a personalized letter to hand clients explaining the price adjustment and when it will begin. Be sure to give them plenty of notice, at least two to four weeks, depending on how often you clean their home. Also, be prepared to lose some clients when your prices change.

Billing and Payments

Have a clear payment policy. I always preferred that the client pay me on the day of the cleaning, and asked that a check be left on the kitchen counter for me. I let them know that if the cleaning went longer, they would be charged and should include that additional amount in the check left for my next cleaning. Before leaving the home that day write a note stating the additional amount they will owe and put it somewhere they are sure to see, like the kitchen counter. You could also create a business form to use when additional charges occur. This form would indicate the additional amount due and what the extra charges are for.

Times are changing, and people aren't writing as many checks as before. Instead, they are using online methods to make payments. Some payment options for them could be to:

- **Direct deposit payments into your checking account …** and you should keep on top of this to make sure payment is deposited when it should be. I had one client who knew that I expected to be paid on time, but she was out of town. She suddenly realized that she did not handle my direct deposit, and called her son, who came to the home and paid me in person.

- **Set up a payment schedule.** You may have a client whose cleaning is paid for by a corporation, or who has been with you for a long time and wants to pay every two weeks or monthly. In this case, they will want you to bill them. Set up a billing system, indicating on the invoice that payment is expected when they receive the bill. Don't delay sending out the bills – if you do, this can delay when the client sends out payment to you.

- **Set up a CashApp or Venmo account** so clients can pay you electronically with ease.

- **Expect on-time payments.** You can't let one client pay you late and expect another to pay on time. Remember, many of your clients know and talk to each other, and you don't want one to find out that you let others pay late. If a client did not pay, I did not clean.

Don't charge clients for a new employee's inexperience or on-the-job training. Understand that your new workers are not going to clean as quickly as you and the already-trained workers do. However, you should charge something for their time. If you think the person is cleaning well enough and is worth half the hourly rate, then charge that.

To avoid payment issues, keep to your side of the agreement. Don't show up late, don't keep cancelling and rescheduling, and always do that detailed cleaning. You have to set the standard by giving consistent and quality service at such a high level that they value you and don't want to lose you!

Finally, always be confident and assured. From your first day, act as if you have been cleaning homes for a long time. Show that you respect and value yourself to others, and in turn, they will come to respect and value you as well.

We are what we think. All that we are arises with our thoughts. With our thoughts, we make our world.

Buddha (c. 563 – c. 483 BC)

Be Cautious with your New-Found Success

As you grow the business and start to get more new clients, spend cautiously and live economically, because you never know what the future holds. A client could decide to cancel your cleaning services for no particular reason. On the other hand, there could be a very good reason for cancelling such as a family illness, loss of job, an out-of-state move, and so on. My point is to protect yourself financially and don't over-extend when the business is still young and growing. Once you've built up that large client base, there should be more of a financial comfort level.

As indicated at the beginning of this chapter, below is a list of FAQs – with answers – that can be provided to potential clients with the estimate.

FREQUENTLY ASKED QUESTIONS

Why do I need a professional to clean my home?

Whether you are a busy working professional or part of a couple, with or without children, chances are there are not enough hours in the day to get it all done. Our services free you up to focus on other areas of daily life, such as work, family, and friends. You may even relax more knowing that household chores, such as scrubbing floors, changing linens, dusting, vacuuming, and more, are not on your need-to-do list.

Why should I use XYZ Cleaners?

We are the best. XYZ Cleaning Company is not your everyday house cleaner. We don't just clean around your furniture and furnishings — we move everything to ensure a deep clean over, under, above, and below all items. Furthermore, we don't hide the dirt – we remove it. We are the "fine cuisine, not the fast-food" of house-cleaning services. We are meticulous, thorough and efficient, and provide a quality cleaning. We may cost more, but we do it all – and we do it right!

What are your fees and how are they paid?

Each client is charged an hourly rate for regular cleanings. However, the level of cleaning requested by each client, as well as the frequency of cleaning and any additional services, such as ironing or laundry, are also taken into account and included in the estimate. A check payable to XYZ Cleaning is expected on the day of the cleaning. A major comprehensive cleaning, generally performed prior to starting a regular cleaning schedule, is normally a flat rate but also can be billed by the hour, and an estimate is provided for that as well.

What does getting an estimate entail?

We meet personally with the home owner at the residence to go through each area of the home, discuss the potential client's needs, and make recommendations on how we will make that happen. A written estimate for the regular cleaning is provided on the spot. However, if a major cleaning is also recommended, that proposal is sent by email within two business days. All services we provide are agreed upon by the client, and there are no surprises or hidden fees.

When is the cleaning scheduled and do I need to be home?

The cleaning is scheduled based on availability during the Monday through Friday work week, tailored to meet your specific needs. We can occasionally provide an evening or weekend cleaning as well. Cleanings that fall on national holidays are rescheduled to a date and time that works best for the client and fits in our company's cleaning schedule. Clients generally prefer to not be home during the cleaning.

What cleaning products are used?

We have a list of preferred products that have been time-tested and proven to get the home clean, sanitary, streak-free and shining. We use products that are not harmful to your furnishings and the home interior. A list of suggested cleaning products is provided with the estimate. Clients purchase these items and keep them stored for use only in their home. If they have preferred products, for instance, organic products, then we will use those.

What is a typical cleaning?

Cleanings are specific and unique to each client, with services geared to their individual needs. However, the regular basic cleanings – usually performed weekly or bi-weekly – include changing bed linens, dusting, sweeping, vacuuming, scrubbing floors, cleaning and sanitizing the kitchen and bathrooms, and cleaning the living room, dining room, and bedrooms.

The major cleaning includes every area of the home, from top to bottom. A major cleaning provides a perfectly-cleaned home with no speck of dirt or dust remaining, and is maintained with thorough regular cleanings each week thereafter.

How is the home prepared for the cleaning?

We kindly ask that everyday items, such as toys, games, books, magazines in family and living areas, toiletries in bedrooms and bathrooms, and dishes or pans in the kitchen, be put away in closets or drawers. This allows us to focus on cleaning the furnishings, floors or carpets, and accessories in each room."

Do you do special event cleaning or provide other services?

Cleaning for special events such as a family celebration, holiday party, shower and other such events are offered based on scheduling. This type of cleaning can be before or after the event (or both) and an estimate is provided. This can also include coordinating the catering, floral arrangements, managing staff and more.

Other household services provided include washing and folding laundry, ironing, and arranging for repairs or otherwise coordinating contractor services, such as lawn care, window washing, cleaning window treatments and more based on client need.

Don't see a household management or cleaning service listed? Just ask.

CHAPTER 3

HOW TO TREAT CLIENTS

Be a ray of sunshine to everyone you meet, and make their day better for having seen you.

-The Secret Daily Teachings

Understanding clients and respecting their privacy is going to be a big part of your success and growth. Treat all clients with respect, and they will respect you in turn. I can't stress enough how important it is to have and keep a good relationship between you and each client – and between your staff and each client as well.

With each client, clean your heart out as I did, and make their house as perfect as you can every time! You have to be consistent from cleaning to cleaning.

Clean the exact same way, in the same order, every time you are at the home. Clients want to know what to expect, and they don't want to worry that you might miss something. Keeping to a strict and consistent routine at each home keeps you on track and makes clients more comfortable in their decision to use your cleaning service. It also gives them a reason to refer you to their friends! It's not hard to keep a good relationship between you and a client, but it does require a little understanding of basic human nature, and a lot of simply being a nice person.

Some of the following points are common-sense in nature; others I've learned through experience:

- Be polite and courteous at all times, even if the client isn't or appears to be having a bad day.

- If you are having a bad day, don't show it! Instead, smile! ☺

- Pay attention to the mood in the house. If you feel there is tension when you get there, smile and say hello, then get to work. This goes for any cleaning staff you may have with you at the home. Remember, we all can have a bad day at times.

- The client may need to tell you about a delivery or service provider coming that day. Pay attention to what is said, especially if there is something in particular they need you to do.

- If family is still there when you arrive, start cleaning in an area of the home that is empty. You could also ask the client where they would like you to start.

- Don't play loud music, even if you are wearing a headset. If you or any employee wears a headset or airpod when cleaning, keep it in one ear only so you can hear anyone calling out to you. The client may try to get your attention and it could appear that you are ignoring them, when in reality, you can't hear.

- When vacuuming hallways, quietly close open doors to any room a family member may be in; for instance, a home office or bedroom.

- Clients are busy people too and don't usually have time to stand around and chat for an hour. Remember, you are getting paid to work, and so are your workers.

Treat all clients the same and never make it obvious that you have a favorite (or least favorite) client. Many clients know each other and do talk regularly. At the same time, never discuss one client with another, and never talk negatively about any client with staff. You never know who might hear or what could be repeated by your employee!

Always communicate clearly with the client and never assume! Good communication is very important. If you are unsure about what a client wants you to do, ask as many questions as needed to make sure everything is understood. Don't worry that you are asking too many questions. You and the client both need to talk - about what is wanted and expected from you, and what you expect from them.

Give the client your full attention. If a client needs you for any reason, stop what you are doing and respond right away (unless something will get damaged if you don't finish it first; for instance, Tilex spilled onto the marble floor and needs to be wiped off immediately). Listen closely to what is being said. Look the client in the eye. If the client seems to want to talk, listen.

Treat a client's possessions and furnishings carefully. Handle every item with extreme care. If you have a cleaning staff, it is your responsibility to teach each person how to care for expensive items. For example:

- Lift items off a tabletop or other such surface, don't slide them – this can cause scratches, dents or other damage.

- Carry rather than slide a bucket of water across the wooden floor. Even a small piece of dirt can scratch the wood if it is dragged underneath the bucket. Dry the bottom of the bucket with a towel each time you refill it – this will avoid water spots on the wood floor. Be sure to also remove any specks of dirt that could be on the bucket bottom before putting it down.

- Never place keys or any items with sharp edges on glass tables, as they could scratch the surface.

- Don't put a glass or cup on a surface without first placing a coaster or napkin underneath it.

- Attach the smooth side of a Velcro strip around the edges of your sweeper attachments to protect woodwork in the home from scuffs or scratches.

- Do not place wet rags, even if they are in a bag, on a wood floor. Moisture from the bag could damage the flooring.

- Don't park in the client's driveway except to unload supplies. Find a place on the street (unless the client tells you otherwise). If any cleaning staff has a car that leaks fluids or looks like it should be in a junk yard, definitely do not park it on the client's property.

- If you (or a member of your cleaning staff) break or damage something, own up to it. Offer to replace the item or submit it to your insurance company.

Always respect a client's privacy. This is as important if the clients are in a heated discussion as it would be if they left a bank statement on a kitchen counter. In the first instance, be discreet and leave the room to go work in a different part of the home. In the second situation, lift the bank statement up to clean under it, and then place it back where it was – without looking at it. The same applies if you know the client or family members are at home, but you don't know where. If a door is closed and you need to clean that room, knock and call out first, especially if it is a bedroom or bathroom.

Be aware of personal items left out. If there is money or jewelry in clear sight, leave it where it is. If you can easily clean under it, do so, and again, put the item back where it was. If you find anything of value that has fallen to the floor, pick it up – and then get a paper towel or tissue to place on a nearby table with the item on top of it so it can be easily seen. Before vacuuming, always check the floor to make sure nothing of value, like an expensive earring, was dropped that could be swept up into the vacuum.

Never take anything out of the house unless you have been given permission, even something as small as a can of soda. You won't earn respect by casually helping yourself to something that you didn't buy.

There are a number of mistakes to avoid.

When starting out with your first clients, always remember that this is business and it's all very new. You want to do it right from the very first day as a business owner and as a service provider. Don't over-promise, don't over-extend and don't forget that the client is counting on you to be there as you have agreed. The following points may seem simple and common-sense, but they can be a deal-breaker if you don't stick to them.

- **Don't take on more than you can handle**. This is one of the fastest ways to give your business a bad name. Start slow at first. Schedule only one home cleaning a day and keep it at that level until you have figured out how long the cleaning takes to be done PERFECTLY. Then you can bump up the scheduling frequency.

- **Don't be late.** If the starting time was set for 7:30 in the morning, be there at 7:30, not 7:35.

- **Don't switch cleaning days unless there is a very good reason (like you are sick, have a family emergency, etc.).** Keep clients on the same day that was agreed upon and scheduled when they hired you to clean their home. If you do need to cancel or change a cleaning day at any time, call or text the client as early as possible, and **definitely call well ahead of the time** you were supposed to arrive at the home. If possible, have a new day and time in mind to offer the client.

- This is very important: **don't raise your cleaning rates if you can't afford to lose even one client.** A client may decide to stop using your service because of a rate increase.

Give extra value by doing more than is expected. Doing something that isn't in the "job description" and doesn't require a lot of extra effort from you can really make your clients happy. Some examples of providing value-added services are:

- The client comes home with groceries and you help unload and carry them in.

- Place luggage in the car if the client is leaving on a trip.

- Put delivered packages in a place where they can be easily seen – usually a kitchen counter.

- If the client has been away for a week or so, sort and stack the mail. Clean out their refrigerator and throw away outdated, old food. If there is fruit on the counter and it's getting old and moldy, throw that away before the fruit flies come. (Think about what you would want if you were gone for a while – it most likely wouldn't be coming home to a smelly refrigerator and black bananas covered with bugs!)

- Now and then, buy an inexpensive, nice bouquet of flowers and place them on the counter for the client to see immediately when walking into the home.

- Let the client know if something is broken or not working properly, or if windows, blinds or carpets need to be professionally cleaned. Have that list of preferred contractors available to recommend to the client. Offer to make the arrangements with the contractor to get the work done.

Going the extra mile for a client shows that you care about the home. It also shows that you pay attention to all the details. Not only will they appreciate this extra value, but they will remember that when it's time for a price increase.

I've had clients show their appreciation for the special touches and extra effort I would provide by giving me little gifts or a holiday bonus. While I never expected a client to "reward" me for going above and beyond, I was always grateful for their special gifts. Even more, I was happy knowing that they noticed and appreciated what I did.

I promise myself...

To forget the mistakes of the past and press on to the greater achievements of the future.

To wear a cheerful expression at all times and give a smile to every living creature I meet.

To give so much time to improving myself that I have no time to criticize others.

To be too large for worry, too noble for anger, too strong for fear, and too happy to permit the presence of trouble.

To think well of myself and to proclaim this fact to the world, not in loud words, but in great deeds.

To live in the faith that the whole world is on my side, so long as I am true to the best that is in me.

Christian D. Larson (1874-1954), The Optimist's Creed

CHAPTER 4

NEW BUSINESS HOUSEKEEPING

Congratulations on starting your new cleaning business! Remember, cleaning homes is a legitimate job that comes with its own set of responsibilities. As a self-employed individual or small business owner, you'll have administrative obligations to manage. Have you addressed the necessary administrative and government regulations concerning income, wages, taxes, and other related matters?

It's important to point out that if you haven't already taken care of the tax obligation part of your business by talking with an accountant or tax lawyer, you should do so now. You are responsible for federal, state and local income taxes, and depending on the state you are in, state sales tax. Find out what percent of your income should be put away and used to pay your taxes each year. This should be done starting your first day in business.

You can find information on these and other obligations on the Small Business Administration website at https://www.sba.gov/business-guide/manage-your-business/pay-taxes

Is your business name registered? In Ohio, business names are registered through the office of Secretary of State at https://www.sos.state.oh.us/businesses/. In addition to helping with the business name, these state agencies are a great resource for business owners with online tools, information on starting and running a business, and much more. If you're not sure if you should register your business name, talk with an accountant or attorney.

When you can, get a business credit card. It makes it much easier to keep track of your business expenses.

Also keep in mind how you pay workers – you will need a checking account. Talk to a banker at any large bank in your area to find out if you need a separate business account and to answer any other questions you may have. Keep in mind, it's not just paying employees, but business expenses that you have to account for.

There are also local, state and federal regulations related to employees, and these are covered in Chapter 5, How to Hire and Manage Employees.

Finally, protect yourself with insurance in case you or a member of your cleaning staff break or damage anything at a client's home or on their property. Start by talking to the agent who insures your car or home and get information on what insurance you need.

CHAPTER 5

HOW TO HIRE AND MANAGE WORKERS

W e've all been told this at some point in our lives, but it's important – trust your gut instincts. When it came to hiring workers, I followed my instincts, especially if there was something in a criminal background check that indicated an individual had been in trouble with the law. The fastest way to lose your cleaning business is to hire someone who steals from a client or is dishonest. You will lose that client, and you will lose all of the other clients that the first client tells. You also don't want to hire someone whose work history shows that he or she doesn't stay in one job very long. That individual will probably not be a reliable worker. However, if you gut still tells you this person would be a great worker, listen to it. People do change. Before you hire someone, envision what type of person you want. This way, you will attract that type of person.

Another point to consider before hiring anyone full-time is that you personally need a clear grasp on how long it takes to complete each and every cleaning task. You need to have this hands-on experience and hours of cleaning first yourself in order to gauge how much time it will take someone else to do a cleaning. This is important so you are able to tell your employees how long you expect it will take them (after training) to clean and detail a bathroom, scrub the kitchen floor, vacuum the entire house, etc.

There is no set formula for how long it takes to train an employee. Some learn the basics quickly, while others may take a few months or longer. Typically it took about a year of training and mentoring before most new employees mastered the tasks and could work independently.

How to Find & Hire Employees

In the earlier years of my business, friends and family members that I knew were honest and had a good work ethic worked with me. In reality, I wasn't in a position yet to afford full-time workers, and was grateful that these folks were all willing to work part-time to help me.

Think outside the box when looking for new workers. When you get to the point where business is growing and you need to hire workers, let people know you are looking to hire and ask for referrals. It is much easier and you are likely to get better employees if you can get a referral from someone you already know. Ask them what they know about the person's work ethic? Are they reliable and punctual? Additionally, do they have their own transportation etc.? That can give you a general idea if the person should be asked for an interview.

Another way to find good workers is to pay attention to people working at places you go to regularly, like a fast food or casual restaurant, retail stores, supermarkets, etc. Observe those employees who always seem to offer great customer service and you can just tell that they are good workers.

That's how I found one of my employees. Jobe worked at the grocery store I shopped at each week, and from the very first day, I noticed how pleasant and polite he was. He always had a smile and gave such a high level of customer service to everyone. One day, I walked into an office supply store in my neighborhood and saw Jobe also working there. I was impressed that this young man was working two jobs.

My next time in the supermarket, we started talking and Jobe asked if I was a doctor – he had noticed my license plate, was Scrubn. Laughing, I said "No, I clean houses for a living. Are you looking for a job? I pay well." He seemed interested and I gave him my business card and said to call.

I did stress to Jobe that cleaning homes is a physically-demanding job – and this should be pointed out to every person you interview. Keeping a long story short, Jobe suggested working with me on his next day off to see if he would like the job, which he did and I immediately hired him. Not only was he an exceptional cleaner who the clients loved – especially his happy smile and hearty laugh – Jobe remains a true friend still to this day. This is a great example of trusting your gut instinct when you find someone you think will be a good employee.

Another great worker was Asaf, who came to Columbus from Zimbabwe. He was on a green card which allowed him to stay and work in the U.S. Asaf was a pleasant young man with great manners and when I first met him, it was obvious he was eager to get a job. I was impressed by his desire to learn and that he wanted to be a good employee. Asaf was polite and personable and the clients loved him, which was important to me.

You should understand that most employees will not have the same commitment to cleaning that you do, meaning that they will have a lot to learn. I lucked out with Asaf – not only because he wanted the job, but because he was willing to learn.

Coming from a poor country in Africa, detailed and perfect cleaning was not a part of his upbringing or words in his vocabulary. Still he tried his hardest to understand what detailed cleaning was and how to do it. One day, Asaf shared his frustration with me over his inability to see details that I could see, like streaks in a mirror.

That made me question how I was training him. What seemed so simple and obvious to me came from years of being a perfectionist. I had to adjust how I was training Asaf and showed him how to look at the mirror from a different angle and without the light shining right in his face. "Rather than staring straight at the mirror," I said, "look from the side" – and he immediately saw the streaks.

That was a simple solution, but keep in mind that you could have an employee that just doesn't see the streaks, no matter what angle he's looking from. This is when you need to really stop and think – does this person have a vision problem and need glasses? My point is to take everything into consideration when training an employee and look at every possible reason for why he or she just isn't getting it.

Within a year, Asaf became one of the best, fastest and most efficient workers I had in my 32 years in business. What made him so great was a burning desire to get it right and never give up until it was!

You can also place an ad for workers. Below is a sample ad that worked for me a couple of times on Craigslist, but you should use whatever platform seems to be the best in your area.

Cleaner, executive homes in Columbus $-- per hour

Looking for a detail-oriented, meticulous and hard-working person to clean executive level homes in the Columbus area. This position is available for immediate hire. The ideal candidate must be in good physical condition, have a strong back and good knees as this job requires a lot of bending and cleaning floors on your hands and knees.

The work week is normally Tuesday through Friday from 7:30 a.m. to 4:30 p.m. However, you must be flexible with days and times.

You must also have a reliable way to and from work every day.

On-the-job training is provided and the starting pay is $-- an hour. Your hourly rate will go up based on performance, how well and how quickly you can do the level of cleaning expected.

The job is ideal for an individual who is a perfectionist, can work well independently and with others, and will give 100% every day. My clients expect a high standard of cleaning from my company and I expect no less from those who work with me.

<u>Must have clean police record.</u>

To learn more or to apply, please email the address in this ad, along with a resume and/or work history for the last five years.

As you train new staff, keep in mind that each person has a different level of what they think CLEAN is. Some workers like Jobe could be as detail-oriented as I am and learn quickly how to clean to my expectations, while others will be like Asaf and it will take a while.

Lesson Learned: *When you find great people and take care of them, they will take care of you.*

Remember: there are Government Regulations

You have to be smart about the hiring process, especially since your workers are going into the homes of wealthy people. I recommend that you do a background check before hiring any employee. Keep in mind that there are government regulations related to employers and background checks.

- You can hire a lawyer for help, or learn what you should know about conducting a background check at the U.S. Equal Employment Opportunity Commission online at https://www.eeoc.gov/eeoc/publications/background_checks_employers.cfm.

The next step is finding out your legal obligations in terms of hiring and managing employees. You can talk with an accountant about deductions you need to take from pay checks and other issues related to wages, or you can check out the Small Business Administration (SBA) for information.

- The SBA has some good information online at https://www.sba.gov/business-guide/manage-your-business/hire-manage-employees to help get you started. This site has information related to both employees and independent contractors.

Once you have conducted the background check and learned that the person would be a good hire and have set up your payroll and other required employer/employee functions, you are ready to train your new employee.

The Training Period

As stated earlier, it can take a year before your new employee is cleaning to the detailed level you expect. First, though, you need to spend time giving the worker some "basic training." Start the new worker's training at your home or the home of a family member rather than at a client's house. The client is paying for experienced workers, not to train someone totally inexperienced in cleaning. If for some reason you have no other way to train a new worker except at a client's home, ask a client first if you can bring that new staff member to their home while they are being trained. As stated earlier in this book, don't charge the client your full hourly rate for an unskilled worker.

Spend as much one-on-one training time as you can with every new employee.

The more direction and training you can give personally, the quicker they will learn and improve their cleaning skills and speed.

Managing Workers

This was the most challenging part of the business for me. I fully admit that at first, I lacked good employee management skills. I was a perfectionist trying to function on a schedule and have everything in perfect order, but didn't really know how to make that happen. In addition, the last thing I thought about was saying "Please" and "Thank-you" to my workers. The thought of complimenting anyone on a job well-done never crossed my mind. Instead, I would point out that if I wasn't criticizing or correcting their work, they should be able to read my mind and know that I thought they were doing a good job.

Needless to say, that didn't help me keep good workers; in fact, some didn't stay around very long. I can't even say that I caught on to my mistakes quickly – it took some time to figure out that I was faulting the workers, when I was the one to blame!

When I finally realized that my management and people skills needed to change, and quickly, I decided to take some classes on how to manage people. It didn't take long to learn that I had been doing it all wrong – and I quickly learned how to do it right. In fact, I took what I learned about how to talk with and treat employees and applied that into my personal life as well. I can honestly say that changing my style of communicating was life-changing for me and made all the difference in the world. Here's some of what I learned that can help you have a positive and effective management style:

- Listen to what your workers tell you. Don't assume you know what they are going to say. Let them finish talking and don't interrupt.

- Communicate clearly at all times. Be as clear as you can and encourage your workers to ask questions. Assure them that no question is wrong or not worth asking. This goes for you, too, when communicating with your clients and workers.

- Never assume that people automatically know what **you** are thinking and feeling.

- Make eye contact at all times. If you are uncomfortable looking a person directly in the eyes, instead look at their nose. They'll never know the difference.

- Ask the person to summarize what you just said, and you do the same. This helps you both understand and know that you are on the same page.

- Don't verbally bully your workers. This tells others that you are insecure, and does no good. It will also help you lose a good worker.

- Be kind, and even if you are disagreeing, try to see the other point of view. Put yourself in their shoes – that may help you see things from their perspective.

- Pay attention to body language. If you see the other person is getting mad because of what you are saying, stop talking about it. Encourage the person to take a break and cool off, and let them know that the two of you still need to talk about the matter later.

- Don't raise your voice, even if the other person is. Respect their feelings and don't criticize what is being said.

- Manage your anger. If a worker does something that upsets you, step back and take the time needed to calm down. Take deep breaths. Discuss, rather than confront the issue. Never criticize, rather show your worker how to correct the problem, while speaking in a positive, calm voice.

- Don't judge anyone, **ever**. Not by how they look, the color of their skin, their age, where they came from, how much money they have (or don't have), their religion or anything else. Judging is wrong and it does no good for either of you.

- Say "please" and "thank you" as much as possible. It never gets old, and people love to hear it. Some good examples for your workers are "I appreciate all of your hard work," "Thank you for taking care of that – you made my day easier," or "I appreciate that you always come to work well-groomed and on-time." You can always find something positive to say.

- Be aware of the needs of your staff. Does the young mom need to take her child to the doctor? Give her the day off. Does another worker have an injury that makes it difficult to do one particular cleaning task? Have that person switch places with another employee and do cleaning jobs that he or she can handle better until the injury heals.

- Take care of your workers. Most importantly, pay them well. There are many things you can do that may seem little to you, but they are definitely big for your employees. For instance,

    - You notice an employee needs a pair of new work shoes, and you suspect he or she can't afford it right now. Go out and buy the shoes, as long as you can afford it.

    - Take workers to lunch now and then to show your appreciation – and tell your employees how much you appreciate them.

    - Occasionally surprise your workers with a day off with pay.

    - If someone's car is getting repaired and they have no way to get to work, call an Uber driver for them, or pick them up.

    - Show each employee that you care about them as an individual, not just a paid worker.

Simply put, make it obvious that you respect your employees, and they will respect you. What I found was that when I took care of my employees and showed that I cared, they took care of me and gave their best.

The points above are valuable tools to use in life every day. It's important to do your best every day, in every way. Encourage your workers to live this belief – and if you lead by example, it won't be long until they follow. I have always believed that if a person does their very best job every day, he or she will never be without work. I have always done my best and have NEVER been without work.

Every day in every way I'm getting better and better.

Finally, never take anything personally. No matter how mean or negative someone's words are, even to your face, know it's not true. It's not really about you – it's about them.

When I began to accept and practice this, my life changed forever.

CHAPTER 6

SWEAT THE SMALL STUFF

We've all heard the saying, "Don't sweat the small stuff." Well, when it comes to providing a detailed cleaning each and every time, you definitely should **sweat the small stuff**. This helps you notice and take care of all the little details that you know have made the home perfect when you walk out that door.

You want to provide a detailed, thorough cleaning at each home – and this includes more than scrubbing floors, cleaning woodwork, and making sure the table tops and mirrors shine. There needs to be attention to detail – and with a keen eye that doesn't miss anything. Is a picture crooked? Straighten it. Is there a dead leaf on a plant? Remove it. Is an accent pillow flat? Fluff it up.

There is no detail too small to overlook, and you can be sure that if you miss that one little detail, the client won't!

Lesson Learned: *People are willing to pay – and pay well – when you pay attention to detail and get the job done perfectly.*

Don't rely on your eyes only – have your workers walk through each room with a fresh set of eyes. Chances are good that they'll catch something you missed. You're looking for streaks in the mirrors, smudges on the door knobs, dirt in that upper left corner of the master bedroom ceiling, a cobweb in the kitchen, or a fingerprint on the underside of the glass table top – all those little things that, if not fixed, can be a problem for the client.

Learn to look at each room from the client's perspective in the following ways:

- Put the lid of the toilet seat down, then sit and look around from that level – you may now notice a smear on the vanity counter, or a smudge on the mirror you didn't see earlier.

- Sit at the breakfast or dinner table, and again, look at things from a seated perspective. You might notice a piece of food or grease from cooking splashed on the underside of the stove vent that you didn't see standing in front of it.

- Do the same in their favorite chair or sofa – look for what may be out of place, like that piece of lint on the lamp next to the chair or the streak on the glass table top.

- Sit on the edge of the bed, then lay back to look up at the ceiling lamp or fan, or anything else that is above eye level. Does the bottom of the fan blade need to be dusted? Of course, be sure that your legs and feet are not on the bed!

Just as important as making sure you've done a detailed cleaning room by room is looking at the furnishings around the home. Was that chair you moved to vacuum under now back perfectly in line with the chair indentations on the carpet? Is the throw on the sofa folded and perfectly placed? In my early years of cleaning homes, I learned some tips about placing furniture that quickly became second-nature to me. They can easily become second-nature to you too.

- Make sure furniture is centered along the wall so that it sits exactly under a picture, mirror or other wall hanging.

- Tables in the family dining room or breakfast should be perfectly centered under ceiling fans or light fixtures.

- Stools at the breakfast bar or island should be evenly spaced, and not pushed up against the cabinet as that could damage the cabinet finish.

- If accent chairs are facing each other, make sure that each chair is angled exactly the same way.

- Check that lamp shades are straight and if there is a seam on the shade, be sure it's positioned in the back.

- Hide cords by placing them behind tables or other furniture so they are not seen.

Make it Easy for the Client Whenever You Can

There will be times when you notice something needs to be repaired at a client's home, or they may ask you for a referral of a reliable person to fix an appliance, take care of their lawn, or do some other needed repair. From your first day cleaning homes, pay attention to contractors that come to the client's home. Watch them at work and make a mental note of the following:

- Were they professional in terms of how they looked and acted?

- Were they on time and polite?

- Did they get the job done as expected?

- Were they honest and trustworthy?

- Did they clean up any mess made from the repair or project?

- Most importantly – was the client happy?

If you had a good feeling about the contractor, ask for their contact information and if they would be willing to let you refer them to other clients when needed.

Do the same thing with any contractor or repair person you personally use at your home, or that your friends and family use. See who comes into your neighborhood to do repairs. Ask the neighbors why they use that particular company and if they would recommend them to others.

Make a list of these contractors and keep it with you at all times. You never know when clients will need some additional help – and if you can immediately give them a solid recommendation, well – you've gone that extra mile.

As this chapter indicates, it's the small stuff that matters and can make the biggest difference!

Make it all about You Too!

Sweating the small stuff is more than just noticing something is out of place and fixing it. It's also about you (and your staff)! If you want to be the best, you have to act like it. How you act, how you look, and how you represent your cleaning business can mean the difference between success and failure. This goes for your cleaning team as well.

People do judge a book by its cover, and people who are professionally and financially successful expect a lot of themselves and those they work with on a regular basis. You are working in a world where appearances matter – and so should yours. Over the years, I have come to understand the importance of this, and I'd like to share some of what I've learned with you.

- Always be clean and well-groomed at every client's home – and make it crystal clear to your workers that you expect that they will be too.

- Keep facial hair well-trimmed (including nasal hairs). Eyebrows should be groomed and trimmed too.

- Have good hygiene, including oral hygiene. Teeth should be clean and white, and the breath fresh.

- Nails should be trimmed and hands should be clean.

- Have a dress code. Clothing should be neat, clean, and not wrinkled. A company uniform is always the best; consider giving each employee a nice polo shirt with the company's logo. Make it clear if you want the workers to wear dark or khaki slacks or shorts, and definitely no jeans. Let them know that gym shoes are appropriate and in fact, most comfortable for the job. However, they need to be clean and in good condition.

- State specifically that no clothing worn on the job should have holes, intentional or otherwise. If there is a company uniform, then everyone should wear it.

- Represent yourself and the company in a strong way. Don't pull up to the home with loud music blaring from the car stereo, or walk in talking on your cell phone.

- **Never smoke** in the client's home or on their property.

- While it's not a necessity, if your car is not in the best condition, try and borrow a nicer car from a relative or friend when you meet the client the first time or to give your estimate. First impressions can make a difference.

If you want to charge more than other cleaners, you must stand out—not just in your appearance but also in your cleaning approach. The importance of attention to detail cannot be overstated; it's these details that clients will notice. The points mentioned above should be at the forefront of your mind as you prepare for your first meeting with potential clients. Whether it's your professional appearance or your commitment to tidying up anything that looks out of place, clients appreciate the high level of professionalism and perfection you bring to their homes.

CHAPTER 7

CLEANING SUPPLIES & EQUIPMENT

In order to give the best and most detailed cleaning, you need to use the best cleaning products – so don't skimp by using generic products. There can be a big difference between the two products – the generic cleaner may leave a film that the name brand product doesn't, it may include harsh additives that leave a strong odor, you may need to use more of the product to get the job done, and so on. (Of course, not all generic cleaners are bad! It's important to figure out which ones will work for you, though.) In addition, I use vacuum cleaners and sweepers that I know will do the best job.

This chapter will focus on the equipment and products you need to give the best cleaning every time, and who pays for what. A list of these items is included later in this chapter.

The client is billed for the cost of all cleaning products and supplies that are replaceable, but does not pay for the cleaning equipment and tools. Each client should be told upfront which products will be used in their home. Let the client know that you want them to buy and stock the cleaning products in the home, along with items such as trash bags and paper towels. Give them a list of product brand names and sizes you want so everything is in place before the first cleaning. Be sure to let every client know when supplies are running low so they can restock for you.

A client may prefer that you shop for the products instead. Keep in mind that you are shopping on billable time and that cost will be included in the next invoice, along with the cost of the products. It's always a good idea to carry extra cleaning supplies in your car in case a client forgets to restock for you – and again, you charge that client not only for the product, but the cost of your time in shopping for it. Another option is to just double the cost of the product which is how I did it, to cover your time and expenses.

Products & Supplies that you provide:

Looking to give your clients the Red Carpet experience? There are two sweepers that I always used and highly recommend.

- Riccar offers a wide selection of lightweight upright sweepers and specialty vacuums. I prefer the Riccar SupraLife Premium R10P because it has a lifetime belt and 20-foot cord, and is 1200 watts/10 amps. Not only is this a very light-weight vacuum and easy to carry back and forth, but it has two settings. One is for vacuuming expensive and more fragile carpets or rugs such as an Oriental rug that requires careful, light vacuuming. The second setting is for the more durable carpets. You can check out Riccar machines on their website, https://www.riccar.com/, which also includes a list of retailers that sell them.

- The other sweeper I recommend is used mainly to sweep hard floors and furniture. It is a lightweight Sanitaire SC3683 Mighty Mite Canister which you can find on Sanitaire or Amazon. I recommend also buying the HEPA #253 filter to put on the back of 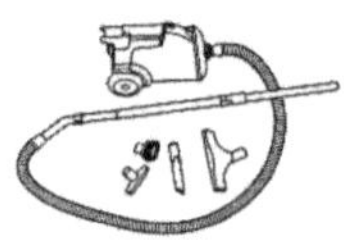 the sweeper. This unit has amazing suction and attachments that work well for vacuuming curtains, sofas and other pieces of furniture. It also has a great attachment for sweeping hard floors. You could also use the Eureka brand; they have the same type of sweepers. Be careful to not let the cord rub against the corners of baseboards, doors, wall edges, and so on as it will leave a mark. Also, be sure to purchase your vacuums locally from a shop that also does repairs on the equipment they sell.

Lesson Learned: *Go to Walmart and buy a package of Velcro. Attach the Velcro section (the one with the soft side) to the edge of the sweepers and the hard floor cleaning attachment. This will prevent damage and marks on baseboards and furniture.*

There are other tools of the trade that should be a part of your everyday equipment. These are the items that you should purchase and have on hand each day. These items can be found on Amazon, or at Walmart, Bed Bath & Beyond or other retailers.

Spiderweb wand, also called a cobweb duster. These generally have a polyfiber head and long pole that extends to clean ceilings and other hard-to-reach areas. Having a 12-foot pole will help you reach those really high ceilings.

- **Microfiber rags** in various sizes and thickness are a must-have. They are lint-free, pick up dust like a magnet, and can be easily washed. **You need at least 20**.

Lesson Learned: *Rags must be washed when you are done each day. You can't start cleaning another house using a dirty rag and expect it to clean well!*

Microfiber rags should be washed only with other microfiber rags in lukewarm water and a small amount of good detergent, generally 1/4 the amount recommended on the container. If the rags are very dirty, use a little more soap. Wash and rinse, then do a second rinse (with cold water) in the washing machine.

Do not put microfiber rags in the clothes dryer. Instead, let them air-dry on a rack – you can find an affordable drying rack at Amazon, Walmart or other retailers. When they are completely dry, shake each rag to get rid of any leftover dust or lint. Keep these rags in a separate bag from the cotton rags.

- **E-Cloth Dusting Cloth®** (Magic Rag) is a square cloth for dusting that is washable and can be used over and over. It is ideal for putting the finishing touches on that just-cleaned mirror or for wiping down the glass in framed pictures. You can get these online.

- **Krystal Clear** microfiber cleaning cloths work great for quick-cleaning of stainless steel and glass household items that just need a touch-up. They also work well as a final finish to a cleaned stainless steel surface. They can be purchased online.

- **White cotton bar towels** are great for cleaning kitchens, laundry rooms and bathrooms, floors, etc. You need at least 40 to start. Like the microfiber rags, these towels are washed after each home cleaning is finished – this is not done in the client's home, but in your washing machine. Wash them in hot water using the recommended amount of detergent shown on the bottle or box of a good laundry detergent. Add a half cup of bleach to the bleach dispenser. Never pour bleach directly onto the clothes or rags in the washer.

You will do a second cold water rinse, this time adding a cup of distilled white vinegar to the rinse water. The vinegar cuts down on the amount of lint left on the rag and also increases absorption. Put the towels in the dryer and run it until they are dry. Clean the lint filter and dry them for another 10 minutes to remove more lint. It's also a good idea to vigorously shake each rag outside to be sure as much lint as possible has been removed.

Do not use fabric softener when washing any cleaning rags or towels!

Lesson Learned: *The more lint left on your cleaning rags and towels, the more lint you will spread around the house you are cleaning.*

There are also a number of other miscellaneous items needed for cleaning at every home, and these are items that you provide yourself.

- **Rubber gloves** to protect hands from being in water and cleaning solutions all day. Gloves also protect from germs, exposure to harsh chemicals and so on.

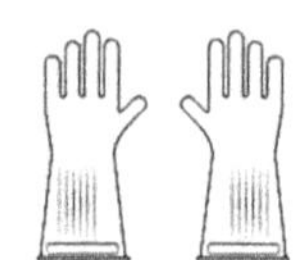

- **Lint brush/roller** is used to get excess animal fur or hair from carpets, floors and furniture.

- **Large rug** to protect floors from the splashed products when cleaning the bathrooms, kitchens, silver and so on.

- **Toothbrush** for cleaning tight spaces like behind a bathroom faucet, around the toilet hardware, etc.

- **2 or 3 old large towels** which can be used to wipe spills, or in place of the large rug listed above.

- **Old, soft T-shirts** work well in putting the final touch on glass, and easily remove smears and lint from a cotton cleaning rag. These can be washed along with the microfiber rags.

- **Scrub buckets, 14 quart** are needed and it's a good idea to have one bucket for each person cleaning with you on any day.

- **Knee pads** for each of your workers. This helps protect knees when cleaning hard floors or kneeling to clean toilets, bathtubs, etc. Note: don't use knee pads with rubber; they will scuff the floors. 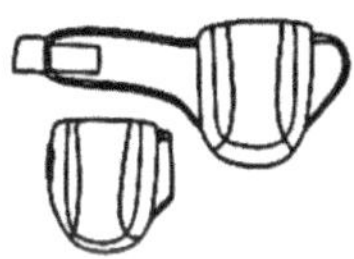

- **Nail polish remover** is a good tool to use to remove sticky glue and bits of price tags you couldn't peel off that were on mirrors, the glass in a picture frame, cups, dishes or glass cookware, and so on.

Below are the cleaning products and supplies paid for by the client, and when and how each is used to clean the home. Again, most of these products are available at Amazon, Walmart and other superstores.

Products the Client Pays For:

- **Tilex® Mold and Mildew** is used to remove mold, mildew and other such tough stains in kitchen sinks, bathrooms or laundry areas. It has a strong smell, so be sure to use it in a well ventilated area. Always carry it in a bucket and place a rag over it to prevent any drips. 
Drips or spills of this product can stain or damage any surface if you are not careful.

- **SoftScrub®** (without bleach) is an all-purpose general cleanser which works well for cleaning sinks, counters, tubs, showers, scuffs on painted doors, baseboards, etc.

- **Toilet Cleaner** (without bleach) is used for the obvious – to clean the toilet bowl. Lysol® Toilet Cleaner is what I normally used.

Windex® Glass Cleaner used for windows, glass table tops, mirrors and other glass surfaces. Each bottle of window cleaner should be diluted with two parts water to one part Windex. If the home has a water softener, use bottled water instead. This would result in two bottles of glass cleaner. Be sure to save empty bottles for this purpose.

Murphy's Oil Soap Original is a great general purpose, light-smelling cleaning product that cleans most hard surfaces, blinds, woodwork, floors, door knobs and more. Note that if the water is looking dirty, it needs to be changed. Remember, less is more for this product!

Dawn Dishwashing Liquid is good to use for dishes and those home décor items that are washed by hand. It can also be used for cleaning mirrors and windows. Remember, less is more for this product.

PineSol® can be used instead of Murphy Oil Soap to clean ceramic or vinyl floors. Never use it on wood floors, though.

- **Bar Keepers Friend®** does a great job on stainless steel or porcelain sinks, stove tops and other such surfaces. Use only the powdered cleaner, not the soft cleanser.

- **Brass Cleaner** is for cleaning brass items in the home. Wright's® and Brasso are both good products to use, and come in a cream or liquid form.

- **Wright's® Silver Cream** is used to clean the good silver, trays, bowls, and other silver serving pieces.

- **Oven Cleaner** products on the market now are fume-free; check to make sure the oven can be cleaned with a particular product. Most ovens are self-cleaning, and should **not** be cleaned with oven cleaner as it can damage the oven interior. Oven cleaner does a great job on oven racks. Be sure to clean the racks outside the home if possible for ventilation.

- **Baking Soda** is used to control strong odors in the refrigerator and freezer. Put   one in each refrigerator and freezer, and be sure to change it every six months.

- **Mr. Clean® Magic Erasers** helps remove those tough marks on walls, doors, and painted baseboards. Do a spot test first because this can scratch the paint.

- **Trash Bags** in 5, 13 and 30 gallon capacity – get a name brand like Glad® or Hefty® that you know is strong.

- **Marblelife Maxout Grout Cleaner** works well for cleaning showers and bath tile, as well as tile floors. This product is great for the grout in ceramic floors as well.

It's a good idea to create a list of cleaning products to hand each client so they know from the start what you need.

Again, if the client wants you to shop for the cleaning products, make sure it's understood that you will invoice them for the product and also for your time spent shopping, which would generally be twice the cost of the product.

Finally, ask to have a specific place in the kitchen, closet or laundry room to store these household cleaning products for each time you come to clean. The ideal spot is going to be near a sink, usually a laundry room or kitchen. Keep this space clean and organized at all times.

CHAPTER 8

A MAJOR CLEANING

A major cleaning is a thorough and comprehensive cleaning you do of the home from top to bottom and side to side before starting the regular weekly or biweekly cleaning schedule. I always recommended to each new client that we start this way and took the time to explain why this major cleaning was important. When you can start a regular cleaning schedule with a home in perfectly-cleaned condition, it will be much easier to maintain the client's home to the level of perfection it deserves on the regular cleaning schedule. If some clients opt out of this, you will still need to spend some extra time to get the house in order, but charge them for it.

Before Each Major Cleaning

Try to get the client to have the air ducts and dryer vents cleaned professionally and then the carpet, furniture, linens, pillows, and drapes. Windows should be done after your cleaning, because it would be difficult to clean the blinds and trim around the windows without getting them dirty again. After all these are complete, try not to wait too long in between the job and when you start working. It will save you work and time. Make sure furnace filters are changed at least every six months and get all the air ducts cleaned at least every other year. This makes your job so much easier; it keeps the dust down and the house will stay cleaner much longer.

A Note about Clutter

Ask clients to put away all of their clutter before you start. If you do not, your job will take much longer. Let the clients know that it will save them money if the house is picked up and organized before you start the major or regular cleanings. They will have to pay the cost for your time if you have to do this.

I will describe the following process as if you had three workers and a lead or a boss. The lead needs to be on top of everything, watching over everything and everyone, and working at the same time. The lead should keep pathways open so no one falls, watch where buckets are placed so they do not spill on a $60,000 rug, etc. The lead not only watches for and prevents mishaps, but also ensures that workers are doing exactly what the lead told them to do – and that the speed and quality of their service is on target. Once you do this for a period, you will learn how long it takes to complete a task. If the employee is not maintaining quality or timely service, put him/her on another task that will be a better fit.

Time management is very important for two reasons: If you are getting paid by the job, you will lose a great deal of money if it takes too long. If you are paid hourly and you are billing clients for too many hours, you will also lose greatly, because you will not keep them as a client for very long. I suggest that when you first start cleaning, charge by the job until you can figure out timing and how long a particular cleaning task should take. Once you determine this, you will be better suited to charge by the hour and eventually make more money.

This major cleaning section is a step-by-step guide of how to clean a house perfectly. Try do things exactly as described and in the order given. You might have to adjust the order of some tasks because of time or because another worker is not available but do try to complete items in this order. There is a reason for everything you will read here and remember – you, the owner, are responsible for everything getting done in the client's home.

When You First Walk Into the House

- Put the supplies in one place, if possible, like a laundry room, so that each person knows where to look for what they need. Next, show each coworker which bathroom you will use all day. I always pick the first-floor powder room, if the client has one. Never use a client's master bathroom; it's disrespectful. Do not use the sink in that bathroom, just the toilet. Tell employees to wash their hands in the laundry-room sink after visiting the bathroom. The reason is that, once the bathroom has been cleaned, you do not want to have to clean it again. Do this in every house, every time. For most tasks, you will want to start from the top and work your way down. There are a couple of steps to do upfront:

- Take out oven racks, then turn on the self-cleaning oven so it can start cleaning itself while other areas of the home are being cleaned. For ovens that are not self-cleaning, spray oven cleaner on the inside. Also spray all oven racks so the oven cleaner can start working. See **Section 24, Kitchen** for specifics on how to do this task.

- Next, gather towels, linens, throw rugs, etc. that will be washed and take them into the laundry room. Start washing each load accordingly and check every 30 minutes to start the next load. Continue until all the laundry is washed, dried and folded.

The following sections cover the tasks, areas and sequence in which to do the major cleaning.

1: Spider Webs:

What you will need – Cobweb duster (Spider Web Wand).

 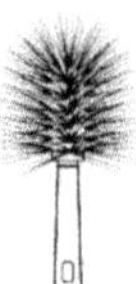

In room after room, put the wand in the corner of the ceiling and wall, and gently guide it throughout the room, getting around the ceiling and going down the corners of the wall to the floor. Be careful not to press too hard, you could leave a mark, especially on dark-colored walls. Get around ceiling lights, windows, etc. Look for spider webs on the ceiling. If the head of your wand gets dirty, take it outside and hit it on the ground a few times. When you're completely done with the house, thoroughly rinse the head of the wand out in the laundry room sink and let dry. Spider webs should be taken care of every 2-4 months.

2: Sweeping

 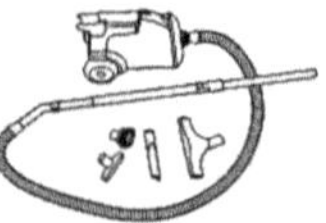

What you will need – Lightweight upright sweeper for carpets and a canister sweeper for hard floors

The first thing to do is assign someone to start sweeping the carpets and rugs throughout the entire house. This will all have to be done again later but will ensure what you clean will not get dirty again from any additional dirt raised while cleaning. The worker assigned this task will go around and sweep all the rugs. If the rugs are Oriental, expensive, or delicate, use the carpet sweeper on low power. If the rug is normal, use normal-high power. After sweeping each rug, set aside if possible. If not, fold it in two so no one gets it dirty.

Now, progress from room to room, and sweep all of the carpets in the entire house. Sweep under all furniture except the furniture against the wall; you will move it out and clean underneath it all later. Once you reach the stairs, do both steps as follows:

1. Using the carpet sweeper, go to the top of the stairs. Just lay it on the step, and pull it back and forth, going from one step to another.

2. Now get the canister sweeper, take off the attachment, and use the pole to suction out all the edges on each step.

Once all of the carpet and rugs are done, use the canister sweeper and the attachment pictured, and sweep all of the hard floors in the house.

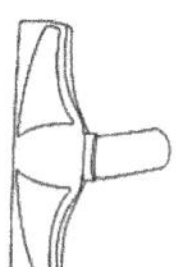

When using the attachment, it should be lying flat on the floor (don't press it too hard) and it should just glide over the floor. You want to go slow enough to pick up all the dirt, and you should always keep the attachment clean. To clean the attachment, remove it from the end of the extension pole and sweep the brush. Do not press down or force it. In addition, be sure the latch on the pole close to the top is always kept shut, so you do not lose suction. You could tape the latch shut to be safe in case the worker using it doesn't know it should be closed. If you notice the sweeper is not picking up like it should, check to see if the hose is clogged or the bag needs to be changed. When either of my sweeper bags got over one-fourth full, I would replace them. The sweepers work much better when its bags are empty and clean. Be careful not to pick up large things on the floor such as sections of dog bones; otherwise, you will waste time unclogging your hose. I can tell you that this is not fun, especially when you are rushed. I just pick up dust, crumbs, hair, etc. I would pick up big items by hand. As you are going around sweeping the hard floors, don't forget to sweep out all of the floor vents. Go as deep as you can into the vent. Be sure not to leave the vent cover off when you are finished; someone could step into the hole and get hurt. Also sweep the return vents on the walls as you go from room to room using the soft attachment.

When you get to the bathrooms, sweep out the tub, around the tub and shower floor, as well as the floor. Of course, if the shower floor is wet, do not sweep it. Now that all of the hard surfaces have been swept, take the canister sweeper and go into the carpeted rooms and use the hard, long attachment to sweep around the baseboards where the carpet sweeper cannot reach.

The worker(s) who will be washing the baseboards will sweep behind and under the rest of the furniture against the wall.

3: Ceiling Fans & Lights

What you will need – Dawn dishwashing liquid, Soft Scrub, bucket, white cotton rags and microfiber rags, ladder

Put the most experienced cleaner on the fans and lights.

<u>Ceiling fans:</u> Use two or three drops of Dawn dishwashing liquid in a bucket with one gallon of water. The Dawn helps remove the grease, if there is any, and is good for anything grease-related. Start at the top of the fan and work your way down. If the fan has some tough spots that won't come clean with the Dawn, spot clean them with a little Soft Scrub (not on the shiny part, it could scratch the surface) and a damp rag. Be sure to rinse off the Soft Scrub before cleaning the rest of the fan with your soapy water. Do not put the dirty rags with Soft Scrub back in your bucket of water, because it will smear everything else you clean. After the fan is washed, I will normally dry it if it has a shiny finish. Go from room to room, cleaning all the fans in the house, including the exhaust fans in the bathrooms. Take them apart if you can and clean the inside of the fan, blades, cover, etc. Once the fans are done, move on to the lights.

<u>Ceiling lights</u>**:**

What you will need: Windex, bucket, cotton rags, ladder, and microfiber rags

Again, always delegate the most experienced person to the ceiling lights to prevent breaking or damage. The best way to clean lights is to make a bucket of water and add about one-half cup of Windex to a gallon of water. Check the white cotton rags and try to find a thin rag. It is easier to get in and around tough areas and is gentler on bulbs. Be sure to turn the light off or unplug it and remove the bulb. Be careful not to be too rough with bulbs when removing, because if the end breaks off in the socket, you will have to dig it out, which is not fun. Be sure and let the client know if you are unable to remove the broken part. Once the bulbs are removed, wring out your rag. Wash and dry as you go, cleaning the best you can. If the light has a cover, sometimes, you will need to let it soak in your bucket or in a sink to cut through the dirt. Once the fixture is clean, dry and smear proof, then wash and shine the bulbs. Reassemble the bulbs and light with a separate clean rag so your fingers do not spot up the bulbs or light you just cleaned. Replace any bulbs that are burned out.

Always have a clean, dry cotton rag in one pocket and a microfiber cloth in the other. Use the microfiber to take any lint off the light when it is finished. Be sure to look at the light from different angles to see if you missed or smeared anything. Never clean a light when it is on or the sun is shining on it; this will cause the glass to smear, guaranteed.

<u>Chandeliers:</u>

Put a bunch of towels under the chandelier to catch any crystals that fall to prevent breakage. If the chandelier is glass or crystal, I use the same product in the water and perform most of the same steps; however, if it has lots of pieces, try wringing out your rag tightly and gently washing each piece of crystal so you will not have to dry the glass afterward. The trick is to find the right amount of moisture on your rag so you can get the dirt and smears off without having to go back and dry each piece. Otherwise, you could be there all day, trying to clean one light. You should go from room to room until all the lights have been cleaned.

4: Woodwork

What you will need – Murphy Oil Soap, Soft Scrub, bucket, white cotton rags and microfiber rags, carpet sweeper and canister sweeper, ladder

Put two people on the woodwork. Ask two employees to go around the room they are starting with and pull out the furniture against the walls, being careful with cords, knickknacks, etc. Once the furniture is pulled out, sweep the area behind it, including the baseboards. Sweeping all the woodwork with a soft brush, including doors, before you wash it is a good idea, especially if it is white. If it is white and you do not sweep or dry dust the dirt off first, you will wash the dirt into the corners, and then you will need to use a toothbrush to remove it.

Next, make a bucket of water using one teaspoon of Murphy Oil Soap to one gallon of water. Make sure the bucket you use holds no more than one gallon of water – this helps prevent splashing and water spots when you carry it or dip rags in. Use the bucket of Murphy's water to clean the area behind the furniture, including electrical outlets, light switches, lamp cords, etc. Then wash the woodwork behind that piece of furniture. When finished, if the floor is carpeted, sweep again, and return the furniture to its original place. If the floor is wood, marble or tile, wash it after you have cleaned the woodwork, and return the furniture to its original place. You can go from room to room and do this, or one room at a time as it is cleaned.

Once you have cleaned behind and put the furniture back against the wall, go through the rest of the room moving and sweeping under all of the furniture, if it has not been done yet. You can then move on to cleaning the rest of the woodwork in the room. You will, of course, need to continue getting clean water and rags and keep them clean as you go. The team cleaning the wood is responsible for washing light switches and electrical outlets throughout the house. If the outlet is brass or a shiny finish, you can use the rag you are washing the wood with and then dry and shine it with another clean, dry cotton rag.

Remember: be careful with the buckets. You must always know where they are!

The woodwork should be done top to bottom, starting with the door or surrounding trim and then windows and surrounding trim and washing the rest of the baseboards as you go along. Make sure that you are getting every square inch, paying special attention to the doorknobs and the areas around them, which are the dirtiest parts. If the wood is white, spot clean with a very small amount of Soft Scrub and a damp rag, and then remove the soap residue with another clean damp rag. Do not put the rags back in your bucket, because you will dirty the water and create a huge mess. Keep a separate rag for spotting and a separate one for rinsing off Soft Scrub. After you have completed one room, move to the next, and repeat the process. Don't forget to clean the wood on the kitchen and bathroom cabinets as well. Two teams should never be in the same room; they will get in each other's way, which could cause an accident and slow the process.

5: Blinds

What you will need – Dawn dishwashing liquid, Murphy Oil Soap, Soft Scrub, bucket, white cotton rags and microfiber rags

Shut the blinds. Next, with a clean, wet rag, try to wash off most of the dirt going from top to bottom. This will make your job much easier and help your bucket stay cleaner longer. If the blinds are in the kitchen, use a few drops of Dawn dish soap to a bucket of water. If the blinds are anywhere else, I use one teaspoon of Murphy Oil Soap to a bucket of warm water. If the woodwork and windowsill around the blind has not been cleaned yet, do that first.

Remember: Keep the dry cotton rag in one pocket and the clean microfiber cloth in the other. After you wring out your rag, dry your hands, so you do not soil what you have cleaned.

After you have gotten the majority of the dirt off, get a clean damp rag and starting at the top working you way down, go from left to right, focusing on the ends and around the strings that hold the blind together. When you need to stop, use your clean, dry hand, and flip the slat up, so you will remember where you stopped. If the blind has dirt that is not coming off, use a little bit of Soft Scrub on a separate clean, damp rag, first performing a spot test to ensure it will not damage the blind. If it is all right, gently rub off the dirt, and use a separate clean rag for rinsing. Do not put either rag back in the Murphy water. If this is a shutter blind, start washing the wood around the slats first, then do each slat. Once the blind is clean and dry, pull it all the way to the top, so you know that it is clean. This will keep the blind clean throughout the major cleaning process.

When finished with the major cleaning, make sure to put all blinds in the house down, and arrange the slats so all would be opened in the same direction.

6: Walls

What you will need – Murphy Oil Soap, Soft Scrub, Dawn dishwashing liquid, bucket, canister sweeper and attachment, white cotton rags and microfiber rags

Normally, you won't wash many walls during a major cleaning, because they can be easily painted. However, if there are some walls that need attention, you could use a bucket of Murphy Oil Soap and a cotton or microfiber rag. If cleaning the areas around the kitchen, use Dawn instead. When washing walls, be sure to also pay attention to fingerprints around light switches. You may also need to remove dust off the walls or ceiling that came from ceiling fans moving dust around. If the wall has dust, sweep it with the soft brush attachment.

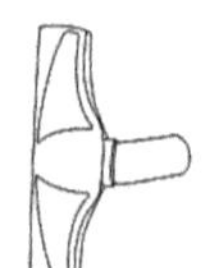

If you need to wash around a light switch, you may not need to do the entire wall. Instead, start a couple of inches above the spots and square off as you go. Try to make straight lines with your rag so that it will just look like shade from the sun. For tough spots, try a little Soft Scrub on your rag. Gently do a spot test, and rinse. This also works for cleaning the wall behind a bed. Make a straight line, and wash in the same direction, up and down or right to left. Go over these areas a couple of times to be sure they are clean. Don't forget to check the walls around the kitchen table, bathrooms, etc.

7: Floor Registers

What you will need – Murphy Oil Soap, bucket, white cotton rags, toothbrush

The floor registers should have been swept out by now. Take a bucket of Murphy Oil Soap. Walk from room to room, dipping vents in the water a couple times. Using your cotton rag, wash them, trying to remove as much grime as possible. Use a toothbrush to reach tight areas. After drying each register as best you can, put it back, then move to the next. Your water and rag will get dirty fast, so change both often. If you walk away with one of the register tops still off, set your bucket in front of it so no one steps into it and

     TIM ROSSHIRT

gets hurt. If the register is very dirty, try soaking it in the laundry room sink for a while to loosen up the dirt.

8: Lampshades

What you will need — Canister sweeper and soft brush attachment, bucket, and microfiber rags

You should clean lampshades before vacuuming furniture so the dirt from the lamp or shade does not get on clean furniture. The person cleaning the shades should use this attachment to gently vacuum dust from the lampshade. However, if the shade is old, do this next step; otherwise, you damage the shade and have to replace it. If you are not 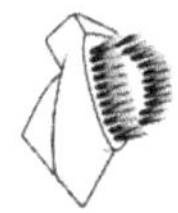 sure, do this next step instead. Remove the shade, and brush off dust with a dry microfiber cloth. If the shade is very dirty, you could take it outside, so you do not spread dust around the house. Then take a clean, damp microfiber rag and gently wipe dirt off the rest of the lampshade. Be sure to get the top and bottom edges. You might have to go over the shade several times before it is completely clean. Wash and dry the bulb before putting the shade back on the lamp. The person dusting will finish cleaning the rest of the lamp.

9: Vacuuming the Furniture

What you will need — Canister sweeper and attachments, lint brush or roller, and microfiber rag

The employee going room to room vacuuming furniture will need the canister sweeper and three attachments:

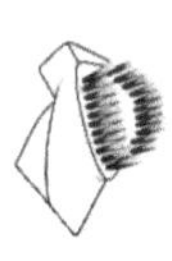

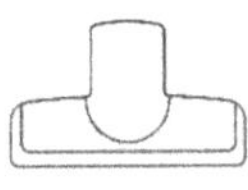

SOFT   BLADE   SMALL FURNITURE ATTACHMENT

The soft brush attachment is for silk; the hard attachment is for normal, average furniture, and the long hard blade attachment allows you to reach into hard-to-access spots. Use the hard attachment for the average sofa or chair (not silk). Start by sweeping both sides of the cushions and setting them aside on something clean, such as a coffee table. Be sure a surface is completely clean before you set a cushion on it. Once the cushions are clean, sweep the entire piece – front, back, sides – everything. Be careful with how hard you press and how aggressive you are, which could tear or damage the cloth. Be sure to get into corners. To do this, remove the attachment and just clean with the end of the pole. If you cannot get in deep enough, use long hard blade attachment. If pet hair, etc., does not come off during your sweeping, try using a lint brush or roller. If that does not work, try using a clean, damp microfiber cloth.

For silk or very expensive furniture, use the attachment which has soft bristles. The soft brush is gentler than the others and will not tear or damage silk. Be extremely careful and gentle with silk. If it is old, it will tear very easily. If you see that it is already torn and you do not want to take a chance, just try to clean it with a dry microfiber cloth, brushing off as much dirt and dust as possible.

10: Bedding (including Dust Ruffles)

What you will need: canister sweeper and two attachments

If the client does not want the bedspreads, dust ruffles, and pillows professionally cleaned, then get another person to help you, and take them outside to shake off all of the dust. Do not do it inside the house, or you will destroy all your progress. Take pillows outside as well and bang them together to remove the dust. Then bring them in to sweep off any remaining dust – if they can be swept in that manner. Be very careful not to get any bedding on the ground; you could dirty or destroy it. Make sure that your helper also knows not to let bedding or pillows touch the ground.

The dust ruffle is usually the dirtiest part of the bedding since it is closest to the floor; you may have to sweep the floor after removing it. Before you reassemble the bed, wash all the bed's framework. It is much easier to do it now than when all the bedding and pillows are on the bed, and you can clean it all much more thoroughly. While the linens are off the beds, flip the mattress.

If the mattress cannot be flipped, turn the mattress. Take the top part and move it to the bottom.

Since you have taken the dust ruffle off the box springs to clean, ensure it gets put back evenly on all its sides. Some people use a bobby pin (hair pin) to secure the cloth from moving once it is exactly in place. You can buy other gadgets to do the same thing. Just be sure it is even, and not hanging on the floor.

11: Making Beds

First of all, if the bed is already made when you get to the house for the major clean, take a picture of it before you take the bedding apart so you can put it back together the way it should be.

If part of the major cleaning is to change the bedding, which it should be, use another matching set of sheets. If not, be sure to wash the dirty ones when you first enter the house, so they will be ready when you need them. The same goes with the mattress pad: For a major cleaning, always wash the mattress pad or put a new, clean one on. Before you do this, use the canister sweeper and the small hard attachment to sweep the mattress before you put the pad on. Most of my clients had their sheets washed and pressed at the cleaners, which makes the bed look so nice. It feels amazing to get into a bed with freshly pressed sheets.

Now, with the clean mattress pad on the bed, put the fitted sheet on first, making sure it is tightly tucked in on all sides. Next, take the flat sheet, and lay it on the bed with the tag side showing and facing up. The top of the sheet displays the design or raised pattern. Pull that to the top of the bed, ensuring all sides are even. One side should not be longer than the other; it looks bad and will sometimes extend past the bedspread.

Take the blanket, not the bedspread, and lay it over the flat sheet, leaving it about seven inches from the top of the bed. All sides should be exactly even. Now, pull the top section of the flat sheet over about six inches until it covers the top six inches of the blanket.

Next, get the bedspread. All are different, and there are very many ways to finish a bed, so I will tell you how for just one type. Take the straight edge of the spread and put it at the top. Normally, the bottom will be curved somehow. If not, you must work with it to see how it fits. Once you have the spread at the top of the mattress, pull it down about two feet, if you have enough. You are trying to fold the top part of the spread over the pillows. Now, tuck the bedspread over and under the pillows, and then display the decorative pillows on the bed the best you can. If you are not the most creative person on your team, call the one who is so he/she can help you. The client can tell or show you next time if you did not get it.

12: Wood-Burning Fireplaces:

What you will need — old towel, the canister sweeper and attachments and large hardwood floor attachment, a fireplace tool shovel or a dust pan, a brown paper bag, gloves, cotton rags, bucket of Murphy Oil Soap, and water.

Lay out an old towel or rag to protect the floor or rug from damage. Remove the fireplace screen and set it on the old towel or rug. Put the gloves on and have a paper bag beside you. Now, remove all the burned wood, and gently place it in the brown bag. Lean the grate toward the back of the fireplace, and then take the scoop (dustpan), carefully scooping up the ashes and very slowly putting them in the bag. Do not just pour the ashes in the bag; neatly open the bag, get as close to the bottom of as you can, and dump the ashes. The slower you go while doing this, the less dust will fly around the room. Get as much of this out as you can. If you are lucky, there will be an opening in the back of the fireplace into which you can push the ashes, making everything much easier. If this is the case, push as much as you can down the opening, moving the grate around so you can get all the corners and behind the grate. Once you have removed ninety-eight percent of the ashes, put the top back on the hole, and center the grate. Slowly close the bag of ash and, holding the bottom of the bag, take it to the outside trashcan.

Remove your gloves and get the canister sweeper to vacuum out the rest of the ash. You are doing this only to get the fine layer of soot and ashes that remains.

TIM ROSSHIRT

Do not try and sweep up a lot of the ash, because it will clog your sweeper and the dust will shoot out the back, spreading a fine layer of dust all over the room. Now, vacuum both sides of the fireplace screen, using the small soft brush attachment.

Next, use your bucket of water, wipe off the screen, and scrub the hearth. You might have to do this several times. If wood for burning is nearby, stack a few pieces in the fireplace; it looks better. Once the hearth is clean and dry, put the screen back around the fireplace. I would change the sweeper bag after cleaning the fireplaces.

13: Gas Fireplaces

What you will need – bucket of Murphy Oil Soap and water, white cotton rags, a large towel, and the canister sweeper

Get the canister sweeper. Remove the long pole and use the soft brush attachment to sweep both sides of the screen (unless, of course, it is glass – see below for how to clean the glass screen). Set aside. Be sure you set it on an old towel or rag, so you do not dirty carpets or rugs. In addition, be careful not to scratch the hearth or floors, because screens can be very heavy. Use the canister vacuum and sweep out spider webs and any debris around the rock or ash. Do not sweep up the fake ash or remove the wood; it belongs in the fireplace. Use a clean bucket of Murphy water and a cotton rag to wash the inside lip of the fireplace. Then, wash and scrub the hearth. You might have to clean it a couple times.

14: Glass Fireplace Screen

What you will need – large towel, Windex, Soft Scrub, bucket, white cotton rags and microfiber rags

Fill the bucket with water and about a half-cup of Windex. Wet your rag (do not wring it too tightly), and wash the glass, letting it soak for a couple of minutes and then drying it. Do this several times until both sides are perfectly clean. If there is a dark build-up on the glass, use a damp cotton rag with a little Soft Scrub on it. Then, scrub the build-up off, and dry. Once you have removed the Soft Scrub and soot, get another clean rag and wet it in the

Windex water. Use this to wash the glass and dry with another clean rag until it is perfect. Be sure to wash and dry the hardware and trim, as well.

15: Breakfront/China Cabinet

What you will need – large towel, Windex, Murphy Oil Soap, cotton rags, microfiber rags, table pads if available, and two buckets

Use about one-fourth cup of Windex to a gallon of water in one bucket and one teaspoon of Murphy's oil soap to a gallon of water in the other. To clean, start on the left side of the cabinet and work your way to the right. Lay a clean towel on the dining room table or any table on which you can safely put the glass and crystal items from the cabinet. If you are using a dining room table, also get one or two table pads, and lay them over the table to protect it. Lay the clean towel over the pads. Regardless, make sure you are protecting whatever surface you set the items on, making sure it's close to where you are working.

Starting with the bottom shelf and working your way up, take everything out of the section you are working in, and lay it on the table. Be very careful how you handle these items because this type of cabinet is where people place objects that are expensive or very important to them. Get a cotton rag. Using your Murphy water, wet and wring it out tightly, and use this rag just for the wood inside the cabinet and around the door and trim. Naturally, when it gets dirty, rinse it out or if it's too dirty, get another one. Once the wood inside the cabinet and on the door is clean, set the Murphy water out of your way.

Wet and wring out a cotton rag in the Windex water, and start washing the interior glass shelves. Be sure to wash and dry the top and bottom of the glass. If you see that you need to remove the glass shelves, start by removing shelves, bottom to top, for cleaning. The reason to start at the bottom is if you started with the top shelf and it slipped from your hands, it could crash down and break one or all the glass shelves underneath. Clean, dry, and shine each glass shelf. Then take two clean cotton rags so your fingers do not dirty the glass and hold the glass shelf to the light to make sure it is free of smears. When it is, place each shelf on a clean towel on top of the table. Before putting the glass shelves back in place, wipe all inside wood with a damp rag if you have not already done so, then dry with another clean rag if needed. Put the glass shelf back, starting at the top and using the same two clean rags to keep fingerprints off the glass.

Clean both sides of the glass doors the same way as mentioned above, using rags to avoid fingerprints. Once the glass shelves and door are clean, wash and detail each piece of glass or crystal. If you feel the item is safe to dip in your bucket of water, do that, and then dry, shine and set safely aside. Dip as many things into the bucket as you safely can; it seems to make the cleaning go faster. However, if the item is not safe to dip into water, then wring out your clean rag, wipe the dirt off, and then dry and shine. Hold each item to the light to see if it is completely clean and there are no smears. Once everything is clean, take a clean, dry microfiber cloth, and dust the shelves before you put items back just to make sure to get any dust that accumulated while cleaning the rest of the cabinet. Work from the bottom up, carefully placing each item where it should go. If the cabinet had no real order or detail regarding how knickknacks were placed, do your best to place items in an attractive arrangement. If you are not good at decorating, use one of your workers who is on this task.

When finished, shut the door, and move on to the next section. Do everything in the same order until all the wood, shelves, and glass/crystal have been cleaned and put back. If you find items that are not glass, wipe them off with a rag slightly moistened with water or use a dry microfiber cloth. When finished with the inside, dip a rag into the Murphy water, wring it out well, and wash the outside of the cabinet. You have already washed around the glass, so be careful not to get water on it. Remove all of your cleaning items, empty the buckets, and check carefully to make sure there is no water or water spots on the table, floor, etc.

16: Silver

What you will need – 2 large towel(s), gloves, Wrights Silver Cleaner, cotton rags or old, soft T-shirts (or microfiber rags), and rug

Put the rug on the floor in front of where you will be cleaning the silver to protect the floor from damage.

Always read instructions on silver-cleaning products. Gather the silver from one room if the client has a great deal of it or from around the house, if there is not so much. Either way, make sure you remember where it goes. A client does not want to have to rearrange the entire house after you leave. If possible, clean the silver in the laundry room sink if the client has one. Otherwise, use the kitchen sink.

Lay out one towel to put the dirty silver on while you are cleaning it, and another to place the silver on when it is fully cleaned and shined. Put your gloves on and take one piece of silver at a time and set it on the towel. Then wet the sponge that comes with the silver cleaner (according to the product's directions) and wring it out well. Generally, you will use about a quarter-sized amount of cream with the sponge, and then start rubbing it on the silver. The sponge gets dirty fast, so rinse thoroughly and tightly wring it out often, adding more cream each time, as needed. Go over every section a couple of times, including the handles and crevices. Rinse with warm water, and then dry well with a T-shirt rag.

If the silver looks great after one cleaning, set it aside. If not, repeat the previous steps until the piece is perfect. You normally only polish the outside of the silver because that is what people see. If you do get silver polish on the inside, though, be sure to remove it before finishing. In addition, be sure not to shut the lid on any pieces that have a lid or cover, such as a chest, teapot, etc. until the inside is completely dry. When done with all the silver, remove your gloves then be sure to wash and dry your hands to remove all cleaner. Then, take a clean, dry microfiber cloth, and wipe every piece one more time to remove any leftover tarnish and film, and put a brilliant shine on the piece.

17: Silver Picture Frames

What you will need — two large towels, gloves, Wrights Silver Cleaner, cotton rags, or old, soft T-shirts, microfiber rags, and an old rug.

With clean, dry hands, remove the picture and glass from the frame. Set the picture in a clean, dry spot. Run the glass under water. Dry with a towel. Hold it to the light to see if it is clean. If not, do it again, or get a drop of Dawn dishwashing liquid on a damp rag. Wash the glass, and then dry it to shine. Set the clean, DRY glass back on the picture to protect it – and so you will not have to match each glass and picture. Keep the pictures far away from the water to protect them.

Now, take the sponge from the silver cleaner, wring it out until the entire sponge is clean, and put about a dime-sized amount of the cream on the sponge. Wash the frame but be very careful not to get the cream on the backing of the frame or the felt, because you probably will not get it off. Once you have scrubbed the product on, take a clean, damp cotton rag, and wipe off the silver cleaner. Perform this step a couple of times, and then dry to polish with a soft T-shirt rag. Do not put the frames under water. With clean, dry hands, reassemble the frames, taking the clean, dry microfiber rag and polishing for an amazing shine. Try not to touch the silver with your bare hands after it is clean; instead, use two clean rags to return the silver where it belongs.

18: Brass

What you will need – a rug, two large towels, brass cleaner, and some clean, soft, old T-shirts – if possible, cut into sections to use

Note: Removing tarnish from brass is much harder and a little more time consuming than silver.

Place the rug in front of where you are working, and lay the towels out, one used for cleaning brass and one on which you can lay the cleaned item.

Brass cleaning products can be different, so be sure to read the directions on the label before using it. You want to make sure that the cleaner will not cause damage to the brass – and you also want to know how the cleaner should be applied and removed. Get one of the brass pieces to clean and use a cut section of the T-shirt large enough to work with easily.

Pour brass cleaner on the clean T-shirt rag and start rubbing the cleaner on the item using some pressure. You don't want to use so much pressure that you break the piece, but enough to clean the brass. Keep turning the rag to a clean section and add more brass polish as needed. Go over every inch, paying special attention to crevices, etc. Once you have cleaned it thoroughly, set it aside, and let it dry for a few minutes while you wash and dry your hands. Now, take another clean T-shirt rag, and rub off the brass polish, using only clean sections of the rag. Once the polish is off and you are satisfied with the results, get two clean, dry microfiber cloths, and polish the item to a brilliant shine. Avoid touching the brass after it is clean and use two clean rags to carry it and put back to its original place.

19: Trash Cans/Waste Baskets (from inside the house)

What you will need — rug or large towel, cotton rags, trash bags (30, 13 and 5 gallon and any other size bags to fit the trash containers), Soft Scrub, and Tilex Mildew

Gather all the trash and waste containers from throughout the house, dumping their contents into the 30-gallon trash bags. (You have to remember where they go when you're finished, so you could also just take a few at a time so you don't forget). Deposit it in the outside trash can or garage. Now, wash each can – preferably in a tub, but a shower or shower stall will also work. Put your rug or towel down where you are working to protect the floor.

If trash cans need to be soaked, put water in them and set them aside to soak for a short while. Make sure the can does not have a hole, so it does not leak water all over. Wet a cotton rag and squeeze some Soft Scrub on it. Scrub the inside first and then the outside. Rinse. Occasionally, you will need to go over them  a few times. Do this to all the trash cans. If some of the "white" cans are still not white enough, you will need to use Tilex Mildew. Tilex has bleach in it, so be careful not to damage the surroundings. Spray the Tilex in the can, and with a damp rag, spread the cleaner evenly across the entire surface of the can. Let soak for five minutes. Rinse and dry. When completely clean and dry, open a properly sized bag, and set it inside the trash can. Grab one end of the bag and tie a knot in it. Fix the bag around the can so there is no air in it before you tightly secure the top part of the bag around the rim of the can. Now, tuck the knot and any other part of the bag under so it is not visible. The bag should only be showing around the top lip of the can. Clean out any trash or debris in the tub or shower. Rinse, and dry.

20: Artificial Flowers/Plants

What you will need – hose with spray nozzle, cotton rags and large towels

If possible, take artificial plants and flowers outside to hose off. You will need a hose and a spray nozzle. Pay attention to the containers; if they cannot get wet, cover them with plastic. Go to the driveway or back porch. Hold the small plants in your hand and spray them off thoroughly. Try not to get the area where the dirt is supposed to be very wet. Once you have sprayed all the dirt and dust off, shake the pot or flower upside down, taking care to ensure the plant does not fall to the ground.

With large trees, repeat the same process, but try to lean the object on something safe so it will not tip over while you are cleaning it. Then try and shake the tree off as much as possible so it dries faster. Leave these items outside until they are totally dry. Wash the container with a damp rag, and dry.

If you cannot clean outside because of weather or other factors, take items to the bathroom tub or shower. Set them inside, and spray them off, attempting to avoid getting water near or in the pot. Hold the arrangement at an angle while spraying it, which will help keep water out of the pot. Shake the plant off as much as you can and place it on several large towels to dry. You should put down a few layers of towels or fold them, so you do not damage the floor. Moreover, make sure you have the towels far enough around the plant to catch all the drips. The flowers have color dyes, and if you do not cover far enough, you could be in trouble. Once you have laid the plants out to dry, return to the shower or tub, and pick up all the debris left behind. Rinse, and dry. Wipe the floor around where you have been working. The dyes from the plants will ruin most anything if the plants sit on a surface long enough.

21: Real (Live) Plants:

What you will need – a trash bag, bucket of warm water, and a few microfiber rags

Go from room to room, looking for any live plants. Remove dead leaves. If the plant is dead, toss it, but save the container and put it in the laundry room so the client can see it when he/she returns. Then, wring out a rag and gently wash each branch. There is no need to dry. Wash the container, but do not return your dirty rag to your bucket. Otherwise, you will have to keep getting new water. It is easier to just get a new rag each time. Remember this advice, which goes with any aspect of cleaning: if your water or rags are dirty, get new ones. You cannot get anything clean using dirty water or rags. If the plants need to be watered, do this when you are finished. Always make sure the bottoms of the pots are dry before returning them to their original places.

22: Detailing a Bathroom

What you will need – old rugs or large towels, rubber gloves, Windex, Murphy Oil Soap, Soft Scrub, Tilex Mildew, toilet cleaner, a bag of cotton rags, microfiber rags, two buckets, and sweepers

<u>Bathroom cabinet(s) (inside)</u>: Before cleaning the bathroom cabinets, you should check if it is included in your estimate. Sometimes people did not want me to clean the bathroom cabinets, but I preferred to do it all when allowed.

Place a towel on the floor in front of the cabinet. Fill a bucket with one teaspoon of Murphy Oil Soap in one gallon of water. Clean out the inside of the cabinet and discard what you are sure is trash. Remove everything inside the cabinet and wipe down bath supplies and other items with a damp rag, then put to the side on a clean towel. If there are towels or other linens stored in the cabinet, wash only what appears to be dirty. Fold and stack all linens and place them to the side on another clean dry towel until they can be put back in the cabinet.

Clean the inside of the cabinet, top, bottom, back and shelves with water and Murphy Oil Soap. Put linens back inside, neatly stacked and group each type and color separately.

If there are towels or other smaller linens in another place in the bathroom, try to keep them all in the one cabinet. Return other items to the cabinet facing forward, with the bigger items in the back and the smaller ones to the front.

If there were sheets in the bathroom cabinet, move them to the appropriate storage space or linen closet. First, though, take the sheets into a bedroom and fold them properly on top of a clean bedspread or mattress.

Do not try folding the sheets in the bathroom, because you will drag the sheet onto the dirty floor and then will have to wash them.

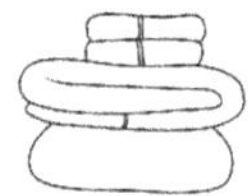

Bathroom closet(s): If part of the major cleaning includes linen or other such bathroom closets, clean in the same manner as above with the bathroom cabinet. You may also need a rug to place on the floor and a ladder to reach higher shelves.

Now for the next part of the bathroom. Get a bucket or caddy to carry your supplies. If not done already, be sure to sweep the bathrooms before cleaning. Use the carpet sweeper for large rugs and the tile sweeper (canister) for hard surfaces.

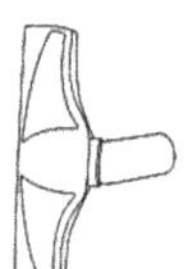

.

First sweeping out the tub, tub surround, and shower floor (if it is dry) will make it much easier to clean the bathroom. The wood blinds and lights should be done by now, so start by spraying Tilex Mildew in all the showers in the house and around the corners of the sinks and backsplashes, if needed. Be careful not to let this drip on anything while carrying. I usually put a rag around the top and bottom of the Tilex bottle, just to be safe.

Be sure to take the rug you use to clean bathrooms with you. It should always be large enough to catch spills and keep your bucket on it. Always keep the rug side up in case a product like Tilex is on it, otherwise if you set it on the carpet, wood, etc., it will most likely ruin the surface. When you are carrying it around the house, fold it up, just to be safe.

If the shower is marble or travertine, be careful not to let the Tilex drip down the wall, because you will ruin it. What I did was pour a little Tilex in a glass cup, dip a toothbrush in it, and scrub the grout until the mold disappears. Again, do not let the Tilex drip down the wall. Always keep a couple of rags with you to wipe up the excess. Do this wherever the mold is. If the shower or bathtub wall is just ceramic tile, spray the solution directly on the mold and let it sit for about five or ten minutes. You might have to repeat this process a second time if it is bad. If there is mold behind the caulking, most likely the only way to remove is to dig it out and recaulk.

Note: this should be done by a hired professional.

If the floor of the shower or tub needs to be whitened, spray the entire floor with Tilex and let soak for about ten minutes, then rinse. Always be sure to rinse off the Tilex once the mold is gone. If the floor is very dirty, scrub the floor with Soft Scrub first, then spray the Tilex on it; otherwise, it won't get as white as it could. The reason that I go around and spray Tilex in all of the bathrooms at once is because of the smell. By the time that you get to the next bathroom, the odor will be gone.

Toilets: Put the rug down in front of the toilet and your bucket of supplies on the rug beside you, ensuring the bucket is always on the same side of you, if possible. Like everywhere else in the house, always know where your bucket is. With the toilet cleaner, spray a circle in the toilet bowl. Tighten the lid on the cleaner and return it to the bucket. With your rubber gloves on, put your cotton rag in the toilet water. Wash the inside of the toilet and under the rim, the top and bottom of the toilet seat, and every part of the toilet, top to bottom. You do not need to make the toilet overly wet; it will take more effort to dry off when you are ready. Next, get a clean cotton towel to dry the toilet. Start with the top of the toilet seat, and then move on, drying and shining every part of the toilet, including the handle. Be sure to pay close attention to the hardware, bolts, etc. You might need to spray Tilex or Windex on these areas if they are dirty. Get every smear off the toilet, including around the bolts. If there is excessive buildup around the hardware, you might have spray again and then use several rags to get it completely clean and smear-proof.

Use as many rags as you need. Never try to clean anything with a dirty rag. You will make yourself crazy trying to take the smears off; it will be impossible. Do not forget to wipe off the toilet brush or plunger, if it is near the toilet.

Using another rag, wet it from the sink to wash the walls around the toilets. You will need to do this almost every time; the walls get splashed after men do their business. Section off the area you will wash by making a straight line at the top and sides and then washing up and down in the same direction. Now, take another clean, cotton rag with water from the sink. Wash the knickknacks on and around the toilet tank lid and shelving. Be sure to clean the hardware for the toilet paper holder, towel racks etc. Clean the pictures on the wall the same way, but make sure there is glass on the picture. Never spray Windex directly on a picture. I use my damp rag, wash the glass and frame, and dry them afterwards. If there is no glass, just dust or wipe the frame.

Showers: Next, move to the shower, taking the rug and supplies and setting them in front of the shower. If the shower has a spray nozzle that you can rinse with, great! That makes the job much easier. Now, take a cotton rag, wet it, and apply Soft Scrub to it. Remember, less is more when it comes to most cleaning products. Use your wet rag with the Soft Scrub, and start washing the walls, glass, hardware, grooming products, and floor. Depending on how dirty the shower is, you might have to keep getting more Soft Scrub and flipping or rinsing your rag to a clean section. Then, thoroughly rinse everything in the shower, getting all the Soft Scrub off.

Get several cotton rags to clean and dry everything in the shower, including the glass, and hair and body products. Make sure there is no soap scum, smears or smudges on any of the products. Now, if you think all is clean, take your clean, dry hand, and feel the walls. If you feel anything rough or a different texture, rescrub the shower until all the soap scum is gone and everything feels smooth. Once you have mastered the shower, use the Windex, and spray the section of glass you are working on. Do not spray all of the glass in the shower at once; do it in sections. Spray, then wipe it off with the clean, dry cotton rag. Then do it again, using just a little bit of Windex on a small section at a time. This will remove the rest of the smears from the glass. When you have done both sides of the glass, get on your hands and knees and look to see if you missed anything or if any smears are left behind.

Once your glass is perfect, scan the shower for anything you missed. Make sure the products are all facing forward and in order. Re-wipe the floor of the shower. If you got it dirty with your shoes, etc., clean it again. If you need to put more Soft Scrub on the floor, just use a small amount on a wet rag. Then rinse with another rag. Do not turn the shower on, or you will have to repeat the drying process again. Once you have rinsed off the Soft Scrub and again dried the floor, stand back to see your beautiful work.

Tub: Move to the tub, put your rug down if it is not too wet. If the rug is wet, get another one or a large towel. Never use a client's rug or towels; use your own. If it is a Jacuzzi-type tub, spray Tilex in all the jets and filters. Let soak for about ten minutes, and then thoroughly rinse. If there is a spray nozzle, use that. If not, fill a bucket, and rinse that way. If the tub is surrounded by an island, start by cleaning that area first. Begin with any pictures and knickknacks around the tub. Depending on the surface surrounding the tub, use little soft scrub on a clean, damp rag, and then rinse with another clean, wet cloth. Make sure you get all the hairspray, etc., off the surface. Again, you might have to go over it a couple times and use your dry hand to check if it is clean. Once that is done, put Soft Scrub in the tub, and then, with a wet cotton or microfiber rag, scrub the tub and hardware. If it's brass hardware, try to clean it with a wet and dry rag and no product; Soft Scrub and Tilex will ruin the surface. Sometimes, microfiber rags are great for this. Make sure you remove all the soap scum. Rinse and repeat, if necessary. Dry the tub with cotton rags until you have gotten all the Soft Scrub off. Shine the hardware and run your dry hand over everything to see if you got it completely clean. Be sure everything is put back neatly in its place.

Mirrors: Spray your diluted Windex on the obvious spots on the mirror, using enough to remove toothpaste, hairspray, etc. You might have to let it soak or go over tough spots a couple of times. Now spray the entire mirror, and using a dry clean cotton rag, wipe off the Windex. Then do a section at a time, spraying again with a tiny amount of Windex to spot re-clean and to remove any smears. Then, to remove lint and any remaining smears, use the special microfiber E cloth to polish it.

Stoop down and look at the mirror from various angles to see if you missed anything or if there are still smears that need to be removed. Note: never clean mirrors or glass with the light or sun shining on them. You will never get the smears off! Shut the blinds and/or turn off the light that is shining directly over the mirror or glass.

Sinks: First, take a picture of where the knickknacks or sink accessories are placed so you can put them back where they belong. If it looks like there is no order at all, when you finish, put items where you think they should go. Remove your gloves, wash your hands with soap, grab the toothbrushes, and wash them with a clean, wet rag, removing any leftover toothpaste. Then rinse them thoroughly and dry. This also includes electric toothbrushes. If the clients have rubbing alcohol available, pour some over the bristles. Wait a few seconds, and thoroughly rinse. Wrap them in tissue and set them aside where they will not get dirty.

Now, wash the knickknacks on the counter, including soap dispensers, toothbrush holders, cups, and so on, with a wet and dry cotton rag. If items are very dirty, get a bucket of water, and put a few drops of Dawn dishwashing liquid in it. Use the bucket to wash the items. Dry and shine each item, holding it to the light to see if there are smears. If possible, move items to one side of the sink so you can clean the other. If you cannot, get a towel, and set items on the tub or out of the way, so they do not get broken. Wet a cotton rag, and wash the walls, backsplash around the sink, and around and under all the towel racks in the bathroom. Next, with a little Soft Scrub and a wet cotton rag, scrub the sink, counter, and hardware. If the hardware is brass, clean it with a wet and dry rag, not Soft Scrub; again, microfiber rags are great for this sort of thing. Rinse dry, and shine. Pay attention to corners, edges, behind and under faucets, etc. Depending on the material of the counter, if it's something like Corian, you can use Bar Keepers Friend to remove tough stains. Always be sure to read the label for precautions. If the bathroom has two sinks, do the same to the other. When finished, check the mirror to see if you got it dirty while cleaning the sink and counter. If so, clean it, and put the knickknacks back where they belong. The team cleaning the woodwork should have already cleaned the exterior of the cabinets. Wet a rag and rewash the cabinets in case they were splattered when you were cleaning the bathroom. Now fill soap dispensers, replace empty tissue boxes, and refill any additional consumable items.

Bathroom towels and rugs: Once the bathrooms are clean, fold and hang up clean towels that match the decorating.

Fold them this way, and if possible, put out two of everything: washcloths, towels, and face towels. Place the clean rugs down after the floor has been cleaned. Make sure that the towels, rugs, etc., are clean. You should never hang a used towel back up on the rack, even if it doesn't look dirty. When done, check your work to see that everything is in order.

23: Closets around the house

What you will need — large towel or rug, Murphy's oil soap, cotton rags, SoftScrub, sweepers, spiderweb wand, and a ladder

Make a bucket of Murphy's water and then set it on the towel near the closet. Use the spiderweb wand to get any of the webs inside the closet corners, walls, etc. Next, sweep and edge the closet floor. If there's a light in the closet, clean that first before you sweep. Now, start washing the shelves from the top down, cleaning one shelf at a time and everything on it, including shoeboxes or other items. If you find things like empty dry cleaning bags or trash, get rid of them. If there are sweaters or shorts on the shelf, refold them all in exactly the same way. Once you have cleaned the shelf, put things back in an orderly fashion. If things like scarves are scattered all over the closet, gather them, neatly fold, and put all of them back on one shelf.

Once you finish cleaning and organizing the shelves, move on to the hanging clothes. Get rid of any plastic dry cleaning bags that are hanging on empty hangers. Go through all of the clothes and make sure they are facing the same way; if not, remove them from the hanger and hang them in the right direction. If the tops of the clothes are covered in a lot of dust, you could use the canister sweeper with a soft brush attachment to lightly sweep it off. If there are ties hanging on a rack, straighten all of them. Once you have the clothes in order, if there's room, hang the clothes about half an inch apart on the rack. If you find too many hangers with nothing on them, gather and put them in a bag to be recycled or donated. Make sure that you leave 15-20 in case your clients need them.

Next, dust all of the shoes and put them back on the shelves, all facing the same way. Of course, if the shoes belong on the floor, sweep and scrub the floor first. Don't forget to wash the inside of the closet door and baseboards if they have not been done yet. Note: the SoftScrub is to remove any scuff marks on the baseboard, doors, or walls; make sure to do a test spot first.

Now go room to room and clean the rest of the closets in the house, throwing away things that you know need to be tossed and setting aside things that are questionable. Many people have multiple products that are almost empty; for example, four bottles of Windex with only a little left in each one. You could combine them to make more room in the closet. Another example would be if there were sixty brown paper bags stuffed in the closet; you could get rid of most of them and put six or so back in the closet.

24: Kitchen

What you will need – old rugs or large towels, disposable rubber gloves, Windex, Murphy Oil Soap, Soft Scrub, Tilex Mildew, SOS steel wool pads, oven cleaner, Magic Eraser, Krystal Klear Cleaning Cloth (Magic Rag), rolls of paper towels, a bag of cotton rags, microfiber rags, two buckets, two coolers, sweepers, a ladder or stepladder for high spaces and trash can

Note: If this wasn't already done, the first step in the kitchen is to remove all racks from the ovens and take them outside (if it's not windy) or to the garage to spray oven cleaner on them. Be sure that you aren't spraying the oven cleaner near any outside furniture, vehicles, bicycles or anything else that could be damaged by the oven cleaner. Put down several layers of newspaper, enough to hold all the oven racks. The reason you need to put down so many layers of newspapers is that if the product soaks through it, you could destroy the surface underneath. Spray a heavy coat of oven cleaner on both sides of each rack. Let the racks sit for at least four hours so the oven cleaner can work well.

You will start with cleaning all cabinets and drawers (again, if these are included in the major cleaning). To begin, mix one teaspoon of Murphy Oil Soap with one gallon of water in a bucket and have plenty of rags on hand.

<u>*Cabinets and drawers:*</u> Start with the top cabinets using a ladder if needed but protect the floor from scratching by putting a cleaning rag under each leg. If you are using this ladder all around the house, tape the rag around each leg to save time.

Empty and clean one cabinet at a time. If the cabinet contains food items, sort through everything, checking dates and throwing out any expired food. Set aside items you are not sure about and let the client make the decision. Sweep out the cabinet if it has a lot of crumbs before you start washing it. Wash every square inch inside the cabinet and be sure to wash the inside of the door. If you have tough sticky spots, use your wet rag and squeeze a little water on the spot to soak for a few minutes and then wash it off. Another option, which prevents scratching the wood, is to use a rubber (not metal) spatula. Once you have softened the spot as indicated above, take the rubber spatula and scrape off the sticky residue. Move on to the next cabinet and do the same process as stated above, repeating as you move through the kitchen.

Now, go back to the first cabinet, which by now should be completely dry, and put the food and other items back inside. Be sure, however, that each bottle, can or container has been wiped down and dried on the outside to remove any drips or spills on it. Organize by matching food types and putting everything face-forward, the largest in the back to the smallest up front in a straight line. Continue this, and when you come to dishes, do the same. Remove and wash anything dirty. If dishes have not been cleaned in a while and are dishwasher-safe, put them in the dishwasher – and wash everything else by hand in a sink of water with Dawn dishwashing liquid. Once the cabinet has been washed and is dry, put the clean dishes back in groups, all cups together, all small plates, etc. If you can safely stack some items like coffee cups, do it. The more space you create, the better. All glasses should be grouped and lined up by height.

Below are tips to help with the various types of kitchen accessories often found in cabinets:

- If there is an excessive number of food storage containers, do not wash them – instead, recycle them. The same goes for the plastic or paper grocery bags we all accumulate and stick in a cabinet

TIM ROSSHIRT

somewhere. Get rid of as much junk as you can, because the more you discard, the cleaner the cabinet will look. Most people do not intend to keep all this stuff; they just never get around to removing it.

This also goes for dishes, cups, etc. Does a person really need a lot of random coffee cups jammed into a cabinet? Don't discard dishes; just box them up and set the box in the basement or garage, for the client to decide what to keep. Also, don't spend time washing any of the miscellaneous dishes unless you know for sure that they are going back into the cabinet. When you put those plastic storage containers back into the cabinet, group the lids by size, and set them under the stack of containers or to the side of them – with the containers also sorted by size.

- Throw away old steel wool pads, sponges, and other cleaning products that are empty or nearly empty. This will free up lots of room for you to organize after. No one wants to pay someone to clean their cabinets and jam everything back into them when they are done; at least, I would not. When the cabinets are clean, put the items back, sorted by size with large items in the back and small items in the front.

- After cleaning the silverware drawers, and once you have cleaned and washed the silverware if needed and its tray, put the utensils back, laying each on its side. This gives you a little more space and looks much neater.

- When cleaning the dish towel drawer, you should wash all dish towels, dishrags, pot holders, etc. so they are all clean and fresh. Some people put used towels or potholders back into the drawer to keep them out of sight, but this can make everything in the drawer smell. If possible, pre-spot and wash the towels, dishrags, potholders with color-safe bleach to remove more of the grease and smell. Fold everything neatly and return it to the drawer, stacked by color and size.

- Never put expensive knives in the dishwasher. Wash them by hand. Do not let them just sit in water for a long time; instead, wash and dry them right away.

- If a cabinet or drawer has small kitchen appliances in it, remove and detail all of them. If a drawer or cabinet is discolored, or doesn't look clean when you are done, you can line it with paper towels or a solid-colored dish towel if you do not have a cabinet liner.

- For plastic cutting boards that are stained, spray Tilex mildew on them to remove the stain, then wash and rinse the cutting board thoroughly to remove any leftover bleach before putting it in the dishwasher.

  Note: Don't use Tilex on wooden cutting boards. Just take a damp, soapy rag, wash, rinse, and dry immediately.

- Cookie sheets and other types of metal trays used in the oven should be cleaned using Soft Scrub or Bar Keepers Friend. You probably won't be able to remove every burnt-on spot, but try to get as much off as possible. When the cabinets that store these items are cleaned and dry, place items back in them by size, with largest on the bottom to the smallest on top. (I'm sure that you are probably tired of me saying this, but it's important to the aesthetics! ☺)

Cabinets with glass doors: Take everything out of the cabinet and wash in a sink filled with water and Dawn dishwashing liquid. Rinse and dry each item. Next, wash the inside of that cabinet using a rag dipped into a bucket with a gallon of water and 1/4 teaspoon of Murphy soap. Clean both sides of the glass doors by dipping the rag into the clean dishwater, wringing it out, and washing and drying the glass. The rags must be clean and so does the water. Using Dawn in dishwater instead of Windex is because the glass in the kitchen can have a greasy film from cooking and Dawn will cut through the grease a little easier. You could also use Windex on a clean cotton rag, but Dawn will do a better job. Be sure to look at the glass from different angles to ensure there are no smears and to make sure you removed the grease splatters. If the cabinet has glass shelves, clean them in the same way as you cleaned the doors. Now, return the items to the cabinet, putting large items in the back and small in the front with labels facing forward.

Cabinet doors and trim: If the team cleaning the woodwork has not yet cleaned in the kitchen, fill a bucket with one gallon of water and add 1/4 teaspoon of Murphy Oil Soap in it. Use a microfiber rag to wash all woodwork. Start with the highest cabinets, using a ladder, if necessary, to reach and clean the very top. If the top is exposed, be sure to remove any dust from the top of the cabinet by sweeping it off if possible. Then, clean it with the Murphy's water.

Wash the cabinets, top to bottom, including on and around the handles, which is where most of the dirt and grease is. When washing the cabinets, you may start to feel the rag drag slowly along the surface. This is most likely telling you that there is a build-up of grease or other sticky residue. Wring out the rag and scrub a little harder to get it off. You do want to be careful, though, to not to damage the finish. As you do each cabinet or drawer, open it to clean the lip around the entire frame and wood on which the cabinet or drawer sits. Use a toothbrush dipped in bucket to remove dirt in the corners of the drawer or cabinet. Dry each area cleaned right away. You don't want water to sit on the wood; it will ruin it. As with anything you do, always keep your water and rags clean. For some of the tough spots, use Soft Scrub and a damp cotton or microfiber rag, and rinse, but first do a small test spot to see if it's safe to use.

Now it's time to start cleaning the major kitchen appliances.

Self-cleaning ovens: Make a bucket or sink full of water with a couple drops of Dawn dishwashing liquid. Use this solution and a clean rag dampened in the soapy water to wipe out the powdery residue left on the oven interior from the cleaning. Wipe every square inch, even if it looks clean, because there is usually a film left behind. Normally there is no need to dry the inside of the oven, unless you had too much water on the rag or there are smears. If there are some tough spots left behind on the edges of the door, try a little Soft Scrub with a damp cotton rag. If that does not work, use a steel wool pad or Magic Eraser. Don't go crazy, though; sometimes with old ovens, they won't come clean. Thoroughly clean away the soapy film with your wet rag, and dry.

Note: remember to start the oven in self-cleaning mode when you first arrive at the home – or ask the client to do it the night before.

Oven racks: Go out to the garage where the oven racks have been soaking. Have a roll of paper towels with you, along with a bucket of water with a few drops of Dawn, and a trash bag or can. Working one rack at a time, using the paper towels start wiping off the oven cleaner, removing as much of the cleaner as you can. Now using a wet rag dipped in the bucket, wipe off the rest of the oven cleaner. If there are still spots remaining, use a Magic Eraser to remove them, and then rinse and shine the rack. You will have to go over the racks several times to get them perfectly clean. Put the clean racks back into the oven. I will tell you how to clean the outside of the oven later, in the section called "Stainless Appliance Exteriors".

Ovens with no self-cleaning option: If this hasn't been done yet, remove the oven racks and take them to the garage to spray with oven cleaner as explained at the beginning of this Kitchen section. With a dry cotton rag, wipe out any crumbs, etc. from the inside of the oven before spraying a heavy coat of oven cleaner inside it. This also needs to sit for at least four hours to ensure the oven interior is cleaned.

Note: The two steps listed directly above should be done when you first start cleaning the house, because it takes several hours for the oven cleaner to work well.

Once the product has set for several hours, have a roll of paper towels and trash can beside you to toss the dirty paper towels in after wiping down the inside of the oven.

Do not let oven cleaner get on the floor – that will ruin the flooring. Put a rug or old large towel down on the floor in front of the oven to protect it. Use paper towels to get as much cleaner off as you can; it will make the next step easier. Using a bucket of water, Dawn dishwashing liquid, and a cotton rag, begin to remove the rest of the oven cleaner. This will take several rags and a couple buckets of water to get it done and cleaned properly. When you think it is perfect, use one additional clean, damp cotton rag and wipe through it one more time. Keep doing this until you are sure that every bit of the oven cleaner has been removed from the inside of the oven. Use Soft Scrub and a damp cotton rag to clean the edge of the oven door – top and sides. If the Soft Scrub isn't getting the job done, wet a Magic Eraser, wring it out tightly and rub off the dirt. Then rinse and dry one more time. You can now put the oven racks, cleaned as described earlier in this chapter, back in the oven.

Ceramic or stainless stovetops and exhaust fans: First, remove the top burners/racks and drip pans from the stove and the filters from the fan, and set them in a sink full of water and Dawn dishwashing liquid. Let soak. You can also run most filters through the dishwasher to clean them. Do not put dishes in with the filters; just wash the filters. (Normally there will be time to do the dishes later.)

Second, to clean the fan, use a damp microfiber rag and wipe off as much of the grease and grime as you can. Then make a fresh bucket or sink full of water with Dawn dishwashing liquid. Use another clean, damp microfiber cloth, and put some Soft Scrub on it, then wipe to completely clean away the grease and grime. You might have to repeat this process a few times to get it completely clean – especially if there is residue left by the client using a stainless-steel cleaner/shiner. If the Soft Scrub isn't cutting through the residue, use Bar Keepers Friend and another clean, damp cotton rag. Once you clean through all product, you will be able to see the actual proper stainless. Continue to wipe away any remaining residue with a damp cotton rag – and be sure to change rags as they get dirty. Finish the stainless by tightly rinsing out the Krystal Klear rag and wiping over the stainless one more time.

Third, now clean the stovetops the same way as the stainless exhaust fans. If some of the black, burnt-on stains are still not coming off, use a wet Magic Eraser, wring it out well and try a small spot to make sure it doesn't damage the stainless. It shouldn't, but you want to be safe anyway. When it's totally clean, dry and shine the stovetop with a clean rag – you can also use Windex and another dry clean rag to get that shine.

Fourth, once the drip pans have soaked for about an hour, they are ready to clean. There are three ways to clean these pans, depending on how dirty they are.

- First, try Soft Scrub on a damp, clean microfiber rag to clean away the grease and grime.

- If that doesn't do the job, then use Bar Keepers Friend and a clean, damp microfiber cloth to scrub away the dirt.

- If that still isn't enough, then wet a Magic Eraser and wring it out well. Put a small amount of the Soft Scrub on the dirty area, and scrub until clean. Again, first do a spot check to make sure no damage is done to the finish. Note: some of the drip pans will not come clean; you or the client can replace them.

Once you have cleaned, rinsed and dried each drip pan, put on a dry clean towel and clean the remaining drip pan burners/racks in the same manner. (Note: burners/racks mean the heating iron rack you set your pans on to cook). When all is clean, put the pans and burners back on the stove.

Glass stovetop: Always read the instructions on how to clean these very expensive stove tops. These types of stoves are very easy to clean and shouldn't take much effort.

Most of the time, they can be cleaned using a damp, clean cotton rag with a little bit of Soft Scrub. Lightly wash and dry; repeat if still dirty. Now, using another clean, damp cotton rag, wipe one final time and dry to a shine. Try not to get too much water on the stovetop. Some glass tops come with a special cleaner; use that if available.

Stainless appliance exteriors: The outside of most appliances will be cleaned in the same way – stove/oven, refrigerator and dishwasher – unless they are covered by wood or some other material. Use a clean, damp cotton rag with a little Soft Scrub on it to wash the outside of the appliance down. Go with the grain, one section at a time. Once you have washed the first section, use a different clean, dry cotton rag to dry it off. Move on to the next section of the appliance and repeat. As stated earlier with the stainless stovetop, if the client has been using a stainless product that the manufacturer recommends, you will need to go over the appliance many times in order to get residue from that product off.

Pay attention to the edges of the appliance. With a refrigerator, for example, open the door, and get the inside and outside lip around the door. Same with the oven door, any warming drawers, or the dishwasher door. Once you have removed all the grease, fingerprints, etc., take another clean, damp cotton rag to wipe and dry it again until all the Soft Scrub residue is removed. Then, wet a Krystal Klear Cleaning Cloth and wring it out as much as you can.

Use it to go over the appliance in the direction of the grain. If you don't have the Krystal Klear rag, use a clean microfiber cloth, wet it with water and wring it out tightly, then wipe off any remaining smears or smudges, going with the grain. If for some reason you are not getting the appliance clean with Soft Scrub, you may need to use Bar 
Keeper's Friend. This should only be needed if they have been using stainless product for a long time. Use the Bar Keeper's Friend the same way as the Soft Scrub, and make sure to do a test spot first; it could damage some of the cheaper brands.

You will clearly see the difference from start to finish, and the best part is that the stainless appliances will be a breeze to clean from now on. Ask the client to toss out the appliance cleaner or polish he/she was using. Clean all other appliances in the kitchen, including counter appliances such as toasters, blenders, etc. in this manner.

Refrigerators: If you are cleaning the inside of the refrigerator and freezer, it's best to do this on two different days. This helps prevent the appliance from working hard to recover. You are going to start with the freezer.

Fill the sink or bucket with water, and add a few drops of Dawn to it (remember, you can always add more product if needed). Turn the freezer off – not the entire refrigerator, just the freezer, if possible. Take all the items from the drawers and freezer shelves and place them into a large cooler. As you are taking food out of the freezer, look at dates and toss if food is too old. If you are not sure whether any food item is too old, put those items in a separate cooler to ask the client about. Be careful not to mix these items up. Put the ice from the ice maker on top of the food in cooler. Now remove all of the shelves and drawers. Keep the freezer open to warm the inside up a bit for cleaning.

Once you have emptied the freezer, and the shelves and interior walls are warm enough to clean without a rag sticking to them, it's time to start cleaning. Wet a cotton rag in your soapy water and wring it out. Clean from the top and work your way down, washing and drying as you go – of course, you use a separate drying rag. If you see a sticky spot, spray Windex on it, and let it soak for about five minutes. Then, wash and dry. Be sure you keep re-wetting and wringing the cleaning rag out as you go. If it gets too dirty, get another one. Same with the drying rag – if it gets too wet, replace it with a dry one. Here are some important tips to keep in mind:

- Always use clean, dry cotton rags for drying what you just cleaned. If the rag is too wet, you will only continue to smear what you are trying to clean.

- Don't keep using dirty rags or water when you are trying to clean something; you will be wasting time and will never get it perfectly clean.

- It only takes a couple of minutes to make another bucket or sink of clean water and just a second to get a clean rag.

- If you remove the glass racks to clean them, take a picture on your phone before you take them out, so you know exactly how to reposition them when you're done.

Once the inside of the freezer is completely clean, dried, and smear-free, turn the freezer back on and close the door. Now, work on the drawers and shelves that were removed earlier. You should be able to wash the freezer drawers in the kitchen sink with water using Dawn dishwashing liquid. "Rinse" the inside of the drawers first before putting them in the clean water. If any drawers are sticky inside, run a little water in them, enough to cover the sticky spot and set them aside to soak for a couple of minutes. Check first to make sure the drawer does not leak so it won't damage the counter or floor. Wash each drawer completely, then rinse and thoroughly dry it, holding it up it to the light to make sure it is totally clean. If it's not, clean it again until it is. Rinse the glass shelves before cleaning and clean in the same way you did the drawers. For tough stains or sticky spots, you can do a spot test with Soft Scrub and a damp cotton rag. The spot test is to make sure the Soft Scrub does not scratch the finish or the glass – if you are sure it won't leave a scratch, go ahead and use it for the tough spots. Once all drawers and shelves are cleaned and dried, place them back into the freezer. Turn the freezer back on and close the door. When the freezer is back to its normal set temperature, put the food from the cooler back in the freezer. Important: do not return the food to the freezer until it is at the right temperature.

The next day, if possible, clean the refrigerator. Get the cooler and put ice from the icemaker in it to keep perishable food cold while you clean. Put everything from the refrigerator (both shelves and doors) that could go bad, such as dairy products, milk, cheese, etc. into the cooler. Then, starting at the top shelf, remove everything remaining, one shelf at a time, setting the food on the counter. Be sure to close the refrigerator door to maintain the inside temperature. (Note: if there is not enough room to take everything out of the fridge at one time, remove items from one shelf at a time and follow the cleaning instructions below before replacing the food and moving on to the next shelf).

Check each item for expiration date, signs that it is moldy or spoiled, etc. Discard any food that is expired or bad and set items you are unsure about to the side for the client to look at.

Remove the shelves and drawers for cleaning later – and fill the bottom of the drawers with water to remove any sticky residue or food drips. Put the shelves to the side, safely so they don't fall. Spray Windex on any sticky spots that may be on the shelves so it can soak in. Let these soak while you clean the inside of the refrigerator. Make sure that the drawers aren't leaking to prevent damage.

Fill the sink with water and a few drops of Dawn, then wet and wring out a clean cotton rag. Use the wet rag to clean the top, bottom and sides of the refrigerator walls, washing and drying as you go. Again, use a separate clean rag for drying – and replace the cleaning and drying rag with a new one as needed. When the inside is fully cleaned and dried, close the refrigerator door.

Note: You can spray a very small amount of Tilex in any corner of the refrigerator that has mold and wipe clean with a damp rag – but don't use Tilex on any other area of the refrigerator. Be sure to wash and rinse all of the Tilex out of the fridge.

Starting with the top shelf, clean the refrigerator shelves in the same manner that you did the freezer shelves, in the sink with water and Dawn liquid. Place each clean shelf back in the refrigerator after it is cleaned, closing the door each time.

Clean produce, cheese or meat drawers that have been soaking in the same way. If there are still sticky spots, spray Windex on the spots to help remove them and let them soak for a few more minutes before cleaning. You can wrap a clean damp rag around a dinner knife to remove food crumbs and residue from the corners of the drawers. Put the drawers back in their proper place after each is cleaned, starting with the highest drawer. Again, close the refrigerator door each time.

Once all the shelves and drawers are clean and dried perfectly, move on to the door. If the door has removable shelves, take them out and set them aside. Spray with Windex if needed and let soak for several minutes. Now, go shelf by shelf to clean the door as you did the main interior of the refrigerator. Wash and thoroughly dry the inside of the door, changing rags as needed. Close the refrigerator door and start cleaning the shelves.

If any shelves have sticky spots that are still hard to remove, do a spot test with Soft Scrub and a damp rag on a small area to make sure it won't leave scratches. If it doesn't, then lightly scrub, rinse, and dry the shelf. If it does scratch, spray Windex and soak the shelf for ten more minutes and rewash; repeat this step as needed. When everything is clean, put the shelves back in the door, starting with the top shelf and working your way down.

TIM ROSSHIRT

Next, wipe down all of the items that you took out of the refrigerator with a damp cloth and use a clean rag to dry them before returning every item back to the refrigerator. Put the clean and non-expired items back in the refrigerator, organizing as you go with every item facing forward and in a straight line. This makes the refrigerator look organized and everything is easy for the client to see. When possible, group similar food products together. For example, group condiments together, put produce back in drawers marked for produce, etc.

When returning anything to the refrigerator that is in an already-open package, like a six pack of yogurt, water, soda, beer, etc. take each container out of the packaging and neatly stack all of them. This will save room, and it looks better. Put beverage cans in a straight line, with each one facing forward. Finally, place a fresh open box of baking soda in the freezer and refrigerator.

Note: it's always a good idea to go back in an hour or so after cleaning the refrigerator and freezer just to make sure the temperatures are operating normally.

Small appliances: The microwave, toaster, blender, warming drawers, etc. all need to be cleaned as explained below. Be sure to clean both the interior and exterior of any appliance, and never put an electric appliance in water to clean.

- Unplug the toaster and pull out the removable tray. Brush or wipe the crumbs from the toaster and tray and remove any food chunks that are stuck in the coils. Do not get any cleaner or water on the inside of the toaster. Using a clean cotton rag that was dampened in water and Dawn dish soap, clean the outside of the toaster and dry it with a clean rag. If the toaster does not come clean that way, use Soft Scrub. Thoroughly clean the outer sides and top of the toaster. Go over it a couple of times, if needed, and then rinse with a clean, damp rag. Then dry and shine. Clean blenders, warming drawers, mixers, and other small kitchen appliances in the same way.

- If the client has a small wine cooler or refrigerator, clean them as you would the refrigerator. Be sure to wipe and dry each bottle of wine before returning it to the cooler rack, with the label face up.

- To clean the microwave, take out any removable rack and tray, and put in the dishwater to soak. If they are too large for the sink, lay them on a rag on the counter, and spray Windex on them to soak. Clean trays and racks as you did glass shelves in the refrigerator.

If the inside of the microwave is very dirty, spray Windex all over it, including the top, and let it soak for about five minutes, then use a damp cotton rag to wipe out the grease, etc. Using a new, damp rag, scrub down the inside, including the top, until every area is clean. For any stubborn spots, spray again with Windex and let soak before re-cleaning. You can also use a little Soft Scrub on a clean, damp rag to clean the interior of the microwave, but be sure to remove any remaining Soft Scrub from it with another clean, damp rag. Then dry the microwave to a perfect smear-free shine.

Note: soaking with Windex is especially important if you have hard, crusty spots that are tough to clean.

Knickknacks: These items generally include salt and pepper shakers, candles, trivets, utensil containers, knife holders, and other kitchen decor. Take a picture of where all the knickknacks were before you start cleaning them. This helps you know where to put them back when you are done.

Make a clean sink full of water and Dawn to wash all the knickknacks in the kitchen. You will first want to thoroughly wash and dry a large area on the counter and put a clean towel there to place the clean items on. Empty containers such as salt and pepper shakers before washing – and be sure to refill them after, preferably with new, fresh salt and pepper.

Wash and dry each item. Hold each object to the light to make sure you got it clean and streak-free, then place on the clean towel. Cover knickknacks with another large towel while you clean the rest of the kitchen, so you do not get them dirty. Leave covered until the rest of the counters, backsplash, etc. are clean.

Backsplash: Wash the backsplash with a clean rag dampened in the dishwater. If the soap and water are not working well, use a little Soft Scrub on a damp rag. Do a spot test, of course, but most backsplashes are safe for cleaning with Soft Scrub. Remember: Do not use much. The more you use, the harder it is to get off. Wash thoroughly, rinse, and dry. Make sure that there are no smears left on the backsplash.

Counters: Start with clean water in the sink and Dawn, of course. Dip a cotton rag in your water, wring it out and do an initial wipe to remove as much of the crumbs and dirt as you can. Try and catch the crumbs with the rag and in your hand – this helps prevent getting them on the floor and spreading them all over the house. Then get another cotton rag, dampen it and now add Soft Scrub to the damp rag. Use the Soft Scrub according to how dirty the counter is. If it is very dirty, use more; if not so dirty, use less.

Clean the counter in sections. Go over every inch of the counter, cleaning it with the rag that has Soft Scrub on it. Dry each section as you go - no need to dry it off perfectly yet because you're not finished.

Now, dip another clean, cotton rag in the dishwater, and wash the counter again. Dry it – but you are still not done. Now rub your hand over the counter, looking for any hard, crusty spots that were missed. If there are any, clean again and run your hand over once more to make sure all is clean and smooth. Once you have done all the counters, get a clean, dry microfiber cloth, and wipe them off again. This picks up any lint and leftover crumbs that may be sticking to the counters. When the counters are perfectly clean, put the kitchen accessories and knickknacks back where they belong.

Kitchen sinks: First be sure that Tilex is safe to use on sink. If so, spray some Tilex Mildew around the drain and on the bottom or sides of the sink, if there are stains and let it soak. This will take off the coffee and soda stains around the drain and in the sink. While the Tilex is soaking and if there is a window above the sink, clean the inside and if possible, the outside of it. You can use Windex and a cotton rag to clean and dry, or the dishwater and a cotton rag to wash. When the window is clean, you should finish the window by using the Magic Rag (red and yellow) to remove any remaining lint and smears on the glass. Now rinse the Tilex out of the sink.

Next, wet a clean microfiber rag with only water, and wring it out tightly. Use this to wipe off the stovetop and any appliances that may have gotten dusty or spotted while you cleaned the kitchen.

Finally, use a damp rag and Soft Scrub to scour the sink. If the sink is stainless steel and the Soft Scrub is not cleaning it well, use Bar Keepers Friend. With both cleaners, use a cotton rag to wash, rinse and then dry. When rinsing, if there is a spray nozzle, use that. If not, get another clean cotton rag, and use that to spread the water to clear away the soap. Dry and shine. Now, look at your masterpiece.

24: Before Dusting

What you will need – Windex, dry cotton rags, microfiber rags and a bucket

If possible, the person dusting the house should do this task, so he/she knows what was done and what was not. Fill a bucket with a gallon of water and a quarter cup of Windex. With several cotton and a few microfiber rags, I normally go around the entire house, carefully cleaning pictures, glass tables, mirrors, and breakable knickknacks in each room. With glass tables, start by washing all of the items on the table with your damp rag. Next dry and shine them, then place them on a clean, dry towel somewhere safe. If you are cleaning books, do not use a damp rag; just use a dry microfiber to dust it.

If there is any item that you are unsure can get wet, it's better to be safe and dry dust it. Once you have cleaned everything on the table and it has been safely set aside, check your water and rag to make sure they are still clean; if not get new rags and fresh water. Wash the top of the glass first. Dry and shine, and then do the bottom side of the glass the same way. If you need to remove

TIM ROSSHIRT

the glass to clean, have someone help you lift the glass. Lay it on a clean towel sideways, and have the other person hold the glass while you clean both sides. When you are sure the glass has no smears, put it back on the table. If you can't do it without smudging the glass, each of you should use clean cotton or microfiber rags to hold the glass while putting it back so you don't leave smears. If you did get fingerprints on the edges, go back and wipe them off; it only takes a second. On tight-fitting glass tables, the best way to remove the glass is to gently push from the bottom up. To put the glass back, place one side on first and have the other person come to your side and put his/her hands (covered by a clean rag) underneath. Both of you would then gently glide the glass top completely back into place.

Once the glass is clean and back on the table, put all items neatly back in place. Be sure that they are totally dry before you put them back where they belong.

When cleaning pictures, make sure that there is glass over the picture first before using a damp rag. Clean the glass with a damp rag — not wet — and be sure to wipe the frame as well. Then dry and shine the glass. If the pictures are secured on the wall, use one hand to hold the pictures in place, trying not to move them. By placing one hand on the picture, you are doing two things: keeping it in place and protecting it from falling off the wall. As you clean each picture make sure it is straight on the wall – and when done, check each picture in the room to make sure they are all positioned correctly and are straight.

25: Leather Furniture

What you will need – Murphy Oil Soap, cotton rags, and a bucket

If there is a lot of leather furniture in the house, have one worker go from room to room, and wipe down each piece of furniture. Put one gallon of water in a bucket with one-half teaspoon of Murphy Oil Soap. Clean with a damp cotton rag. If there aren't many leather furnishings, have the worker who is handling the dusting clean these pieces as he/she goes. Some sofas and chairs will come apart for cleaning; others will not. Be sure to get between and behind the cushions if they do not. Wash all sides. Those areas that are very dirty will need to be wiped down several times. Be careful that you do not scrub so hard that you will destroy the surface.

26: Dusting

What you will need – Murphy Oil Soap, Windex (in case you see anything that was missed), cotton and microfiber rags, and a bucket

Fill your bucket with 1/2 teaspoon of Murphy's Oil Soup and a gallon of water. Hang the bottle of Windex over the middle of your bucket but be careful to not let it slide down to one end. Remember to do this, otherwise, the weight of the bottle of Windex could cause the bucket of water to tip over and spill.

Start with the upstairs first. Tightly wring out your wet rag, and start at the top with each piece of furniture. Remove everything on top and set it aside; generally, you should be able to put these items on the floor. Use this same rag only for dusting the tops of furniture – that is where there is the most dust. Do not put this rag back in the water so the water does not get dirty. Get a new clean rag when needed. When the top of the furniture is clean, use another clean rag, wring it out tightly, and wash the entire piece of furniture, paying attention to any handles or knobs and the area around them. If the piece of furniture is very dirty, repeat the cleaning process to make sure you get all the dust off.

Now, wring out the second rag (again, get a clean one if it's dirty) and wipe off, dry and shine the items that go back on the furniture, if they have not already been cleaned. Do the same steps to every piece of furniture in each room. Be careful not to put anything that is still wet back on the furniture and be sure the top of the furniture is completely dry before you put anything back on it. Don't forget to clean the base of all lamps.

As you go around the room, check to make sure all lampshades and pictures are straight, pillows are perfectly fluffed and positioned properly. Finally, make sure all the furniture is back in its original place. As you leave the room, take one more look to see if you missed anything. Now the only thing that should be left to be done in the room is either sweeping the carpet and/or scrubbing the floor. Go from room to room throughout the house in the same manner.

27: Outside Entrance

What you will need – Broom

Have someone go outside each door of the house to sweep the porch and sidewalk so that dirt will not get tracked back in the house. Do this for all doors, especially the garage and mudroom. Shake or otherwise clean any rugs that are outside by each door.

28: Finishing the House

What you will need – both sweepers, Murphy Oil Soap, Pine Sol (or other floor cleaner for ceramic floors), cotton and microfiber rags, knee pads, and a bucket

Sweep all of the rugs in the house again and fold them in half if possible – this keeps the top of the rug clean. Also, sweep all of the hard floors again. Now it is time to scrub the floors. Make a bucket of water and Murphy Oil soap. You also need a couple of cotton rags and microfiber rags for this. Murphy Oil Soap can be used on most any floor, including marble; however, on marble and shiny surfaces, you will need to wring your rag out a little tighter, so it does not leave water spots behind. It's best to dry as you go with shining marble floors to help prevent spotting.

Put your knee pads on and go to the top floor. When scrubbing the floors, don't brace yourself with one hand directly on the floor as you scrub – especially on an area you just cleaned. This will leave handprints. Instead, place a clean microfiber rag on the floor under your hand – and move the rag each time you move your hand. You would also use this rag as you are scrubbing to wipe off any dust you may see still on the baseboards. FYI, this takes a little pressure off of your arm as well.

Start your scrubbing with the bathroom and bedroom floors, and then the hall and steps. Wring your rag out often, leaving it wet enough to cut through the dirt, but not so wet that it takes longer than sixty seconds to dry. Clean from right to left, and only do as much as you can reach in each section. Use the edges of baseboards or the edge of a doorway as a marker for each section you are working on – this helps you know what you have done and what you still have to do. Just a reminder: if you are right-handed, keep your bucket to your right side, and if you are left-handed, then keep it on the left side. As you are scrubbing the floors, always slide the bucket with you, making sure you are not scratching the floor with the bottom of the bucket. It's a good idea to always keep a dry towel or rag under the bucket to prevent this. Keeping the bucket close to you also prevents wasted time as you don't have to keep getting up and down to wring out the rag. By the way, this also helps prevent putting extra pressure on your body and knees from getting up and down a lot. When cleaning the floor, you need to put enough pressure to get the dirt off, but not so much that it will tire you after one room. Here are a few tips to keep in mind:

- Be sure to change your water and get clean rags when the others are dirty.

- Scrub every inch of the floor and don't forget the corners.

- If this is your first time cleaning this particular house, you should go over all floors two or three times to be sure you got them completely clean.

When you are done scrubbing and the floors are dry, carefully put all rugs back in place. Wipe away any dust or dirt that fell to the floor from the rugs as you go.

Once the top floor is completed, then move on to the basement, if there is one. The first floor is always done last. Scrub floors on each level of the home in the same manner as explained above.

29: Laundry Room (Or whichever room you have been filling buckets, keeping your supplies, etc.)

What you will need – Soft Scrub, Bar Keepers Friend, cotton and microfiber rags, knee pads, and a bucket

If the washer and dryer is in this room and you were doing laundry during the day, do not clean woodwork until the last load is taken out of the dryer and folded. If it is physically possible, pull out the washer and dryer to clean walls, hoses and drains, flooring, etc. behind them. When putting the appliances back in place, make sure the washer hose is back securely in the drain. Then check to make sure the dryer vent is properly attached when you put the dryer back. This is important because if the dryer vent is not properly attached, your now perfectly clean house will be very dusty the next time you arrive. If there seems to be a problem, let the client know and offer to call a handyman to secure the dryer vent. The client may already have a preferred handyman, but if not, let them know that you have a list of reliable contractors that you could call.

Note: if you call a handyman for repairs or work, this is at the client's expense. You can pay upfront and then bill the client, or simply have the person bill the client. Check to see what the client prefers.

Now clean the lint trap on the dryer, then clean the outside, top and sides, of the washer and dryer with a damp rag. Use Soft Scrub if the damp rag isn't getting the job done and be sure to dry as you go. Clean inside the washer door, using a toothbrush for tough-to-reach areas. Clean inside the tub as well. If there is a ring from residue, use just a little Soft Scrub to remove it, but be sure to rinse very thoroughly. When you are done cleaning the inside of the washer, set it to rinse and run to make sure all cleaning product and residue is removed.

If laundry room cabinets are Formica or laminate, use a tiny amount of Soft Scrub and a damp rag to wash, rinse, dry, and shine them to remove all smears and film. Do the same for the counters if it is safe to use Soft Scrub on them. If you're not sure which product to use, wash with a damp rag and dry thoroughly. Be sure everything on the counter has been picked up and cleaned behind and underneath. If clean clothes are on the counter but not yet folded, fold them neatly, and group together in matching order. If there were clothes already in the dryer when you started cleaning, be sure to fold them as well.

Clean and wash all pictures, knickknacks, etc. in the laundry room the same way you did when dusting.

The last thing you are going to do in the laundry room is to scour the sink with Soft Scrub or Bar Keepers Friend if it is stainless steel. Rinse, dry, and shine. However, you only do this last step when every other task and cleaning project has been finished in the house, every worker's hands have been washed and no one needs to use the sink, and you are all ready to walk out the door.

The Final Look:

What you will need – sweepers, cotton and microfiber rags, and hair pick

The lead does the final walk-through of the house, making sure of the following:

- Everything is put back in the proper place and position – this includes furniture, knickknacks, home décor accessories, etc.

- Pictures are straight on the walls,

- Beds are made perfectly,

- All pillows are fluffed and positioned in the right place

- Any candles are straight

- Bathroom rugs down, clean towels out, and the first sheet of toilet paper is folded, etc.

Now you start a final sweeping using the carpet sweeper. Do the second-floor carpet first, starting at the far end of each room, working your way back out the door. If the room has a rug with tassels, use a hair pick to neatly comb through them, straightening any tangles so they are all going in the same direction.

Use a damp rag to wipe away any dust or dirt that came from combing. Keep the sweeper lines as straight as you can and turn off the lights in each room as you leave. I always do a quick look in the room so I can admire all of our hard work! ☺ Don't forget to put all of the blinds down and open them slightly, all over the house.

Do this in each room, leaving the hall and stairs for last. Once everything is in order on the upstairs floor and the lights are off, vacuum the hall carpets and stairs one last time. Repeat these steps throughout the rest of the house – but do so in such a way that you are heading out the door, if possible and not leaving tracks on what you just vacuumed or swept. For example, if you leave the home through the laundry room, do that room last, so no one messes up what has been cleaned or needs to walk on the carpet you just swept to leave. Note: make sure that all exterior doors are locked as you do so.

If the kitchen counters need to be dusted again (and you can have another worker do this as you are sweeping), use a clean dry microfiber rag. The reason for this is that the counters can get dusty from all the movement in the house and in the kitchen. The person who cleaned the bathrooms should check the powder room and reclean the toilet that everyone has been using all day. Remember to fold the first square of toilet paper as follows: fold it into an arrow, folding the corners of each side inward to form a pointed tip. Position the folded paper neatly down with the point at the bottom (like an upside-down arrow). 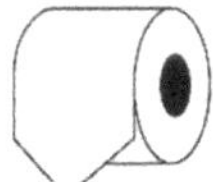

Once everything has been done and the laundry room sink has been dried out, gather your things, congratulate everyone on the amazing job they did, set the alarm, lock the door, and celebrate!

CHAPTER 9

THE REGULAR CLEANING

The major cleaning is done, and you have spent numerous hours and most likely more than one day completing the major cleaning. The home is spotless and in perfect order – and you have laid the groundwork that will make it easier to clean and maintain the home with the regular weekly or bi-weekly cleanings.

Ready to Roll with the Regular Cleanings

A regular cleaning is similar to a major cleaning – only you're doing a lot less. When you first walk into a house, put your supplies down and greet the clients if they are there. Have your partner start on the bathrooms while you gather all the trash from around the house and start scoping things out, looking to see how bad it is so that you can judge how much time the cleaning will take and how much time you will need for each task. If it's exceptionally dirty, you will have to make a few shortcuts to keep to your scheduled time. Shortcuts can include dusting just the tops of a piece of furniture, instead of the entire thing, and skipping the dining room if no one has even walked in there – in other words, small things that the client will not even notice you've skipped. Next week, if the house is not too dirty, you can take care of the things you skipped the week before. You will also need to keep up on the extras, such as baseboards, blinds, etc. I normally take advantage of these things when the client is out of town or their kids are in college for the school year because that's when I can get through the regular tasks quickly and concentrate on the extra stuff. I highly recommend that you ask your clients to keep you on the schedule even when they are on vacation so that you can take care of the extras. If not, they will be paying for them anyway when you have to schedule extra time to do them.

I'll first give you a list of how the day should go (some of which you may recognize from the previous paragraph), and then I'll give you details on how to get it done. (Note: a lot of this chapter is a repeat from the last one, but I feel it is important to include so you do not have to refer back to the last chapter to complete a regular cleaning).

Order of Cleaning:

1. Greet clients.

2. If you haven't done so already, shake all rags you plan to use outside before starting to clean.

3. Scope out the house while emptying the trash to see how long things are going to take to complete and organize the house as you go.

4. Start on the bathrooms.

5. Gather sheets, towels rugs, etc. to be washed and start the wash.

6. Put clean linens on the beds.

7. Vacuum rugs that are on the hard floors and sweep all the hard floors around the house.

8. Check laundry.

9. Start dusting the house (I normally start from the top floor and go down).

10. Start scrubbing floors.

11. Fold laundry and hang clean towels after bathrooms are clean.

12. Clean kitchen.

13. Put rugs down.

14. Vacuum carpets and make sure everything is in its place.

15. Sweep exterior walkways, including the entrance to the garage(s) and mud rooms.

16. Touch up the powder room you've been using throughout the day.

17. Clean laundry room (where you have been filling buckets, etc.).

18. Do one more scan of the house, making sure you have all your supplies, everything is in perfect order, and all doors are locked, lights off, etc.

19. Leave, turning on alarm if required.

Before You Get Started on the Details

1. Gather trash around the house.

2. While seeing what needs to be done, gather the towels, rugs, and sheets that need to be washed and tidy up and organize the house as you go.

3. Start the laundry and then check it often to make sure it all gets done before you are finished.

Sweeping Floors:

1. First, go around and sweep all of the rugs and carpets on the hard floors, using the carpet vacuum.

2. If there are oriental rugs or expensive, delicate rugs, use the low power of the carpet sweeper, but if it is just a normal rug, use the high power. Be sure to lift up the rugs once in a while to clean underneath them, every two weeks if possible.

3. Once you have done that, get the canister sweeper and this attachment…

    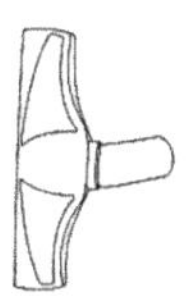

    … and sweep all of the hard floors in the entire house. You want to go slowly enough to pick up all of the dirt, and the attachment should be kept clean at all times. Take the attachment off once in a while and use the end of the pole to sweep the brushes off. When sweeping, the attachment should be lying flat on the floor and it should just glide over it – don't press down or force it. Also, be sure that the latch on the pole close to the top is kept closed at all times so that you don't lose suction. (I normally tape the latch closed in case someone uses it who does not know that it has to be closed.)

4. If you notice that the sweeper is not picking up like it's supposed to, check to see if the hose is clogged or the bag needs to be changed. (When either of my sweeper bags got over one-fourth full, I would empty it.) The sweepers work a lot better when the bags are empty and clean. Be careful not to pick up large things on the floor, such as sections of dog bones, etc. Otherwise, you will spend time trying to unclog your hose, and I can tell you, this is not fun, especially when you are rushed! Just pick up dust, crumbs, hair, etc. with the sweeper and pick up the big stuff by hand as you are sweeping. When sweeping, don't forget to sweep the bathroom; the showers, tub, surrounding areas, etc.

Cleaning Bathrooms

1. Bathrooms should be swept first, before being cleaned, to remove hair and dust to make your job a lot easier.

2. Gather supplies needed: Windex, Tilex, Soft Scrub, toilet cleaner, cotton rags, microfiber rags, a finishing rag for mirrors, rug, and rubber gloves. Put these supplies in your bucket.

3. Go around to each bathroom and spray Tilex in the showers on the mold. Be careful not to let the Tilex drip down the wall so it doesn't cause damage.

4. Toilet:

    a. Put the rug down in front of the toilet and place your bucket of supplies on the rug next to you, making sure the bucket is always on the same side of you, if possible. (Wherever you are in the house, you should know which side your bucket is on. As a reminder, I'm right handed, so I always kept my bucket on the right side of me.)

b. Take the toilet cleaner and spray a circle of the product in the toilet bowl. Tighten the lid on the cleaner and put it back into the bucket.

c. Put your rubber gloves on, take a cotton rag, and stick it into the water. Wash the inside of the toilet first, then the top and bottom of the toilet seat, followed by every part of the toilet, from top to bottom. You don't want to make the toilet super wet because it will take more effort to dry it off when you're ready.

d. Next, get a clean cotton towel to dry the toilet. Start with the top of the toilet seat and then move on, drying and polishing every part of the toilet, including the handle. Be sure to pay close attention to the hardware, bolts, etc. You might need to spray Tilex or Windex on these areas if they are very dirty. Get every smear off the toilet, including around the bolts and caps. If there is a lot of build up around the hardware, you might have to use several rags to get it completely clean and smear-free. Use as many rags as you need. Don't ever try to clean anything with a dirty rag – you will make yourself crazy trying to take the smears off, and it will be impossible. Don't forget to wash the toilet brush or plunger if it's near the toilet.

e. Using a clean rag, wet it from the sink to wash and dry the hardware around the toilet, including the toilet paper holder, towel racks, etc. and the walls around the toilets. You will need to do this almost every time because the walls get splashed when men do their business. Section off the area you are going to wash by making a straight line at the top and sides and then wash up and down in the same direction. Don't forget to fold the first sheet of the toilet paper and replace the toilet paper roll if it's almost gone. Put the left-over roll of toilet paper on top of the new one.

5. Shower:

a. Short cut:

i. Put your rug and supplies down in front of the shower. If you clean the shower once a week and it's not that dirty, try to clean it without turning on the water it saves a lot of time.

ii. Use a cotton rag with a little Soft Scrub on a damp rag and scrub the bottom one-fourth of the shower and glass doors, drying off with a separate clean rag as you go (the soap scum is usually on the lower parts of the shower).

iii. Next, working in sections, take another clean, damp microfiber rag and again wipe off all the walls and glass to remove any additional residue, drying with a separate cotton rag as you go.

iv. Wring your rag out and clean and shine the fixtures.

v. Then quickly wipe off the shelves and products on them. Place the products facing forward, with the largest in back to smallest in front.

vi. Use a clean cotton rag and Windex to clean and shine both sides of the glass.

vii. Do the same process shown in steps ii) and iii) above to clean and dry the shower floor. Be careful to not splash soap or water onto the already cleaned glass doors – and if there are splatters, be sure to remove them.

b. Full cleaning of the shower:

i. Take your rug and supplies and set them in front of the shower door. If the shower has a spray nozzle that you are able to rinse with, great! It makes it a lot easier for you.

ii. Take a cotton rag, wet it, and put some Soft Scrub on it. Remember, less is more when it comes to most cleaning products. Use your wet rag and start washing the walls, glass, products, hardware, and floor. Depending on how dirty the shower is, you might have to keep getting more Soft Scrub and flipping or rinsing your rag to a clean section.

iii. Then, thoroughly rinse down the shower, getting all of the Soft Scrub off the wall, products, etc. and rinsing it down the drain.

iv. Next, get several cotton rags and dry the shower, including the glass and shower products. Make sure everything is smear-free, except for the glass – up to this point, you should have just been getting the soap scum off.

   v.   If you think that all of the walls are clean with no smears, take your clean, dry hand and feel the walls. If you feel anything rough or of a different texture, then re-scrub the shower until all of the soap scum is gone.

   vi.   Once you have mastered the shower, use the Windex and spray the section of glass you are working on. Start at the top and work down. Don't spray all the glass in the shower at once – just do sections. Spray and then wipe it off with the clean, dry cotton rag. Then do it again, using just a little bit of Windex, a section at a time. This will take the rest of the smears out of the glass. When you have done both sides of the glass, get on your hands and knees and look up to see if you missed anything, or if there are any smears left behind.

   vii.   Once your glass is perfect, scan the shower for anything you could have missed and make sure the products are all facing forward and in order.

   viii.   Re-wipe the floor in the shower if you got it dirty with your shoes. If you need to put Soft Scrub on the floor again, just use a small amount with a wet rag. Then, rinse with another rag. Don't turn on the water in the shower again, or you will have to do it all again.

6.   Tub (quick clean if it has not been used):

   a.   Put your rug down in front of the tub; if the rug has become too wet from cleaning the shower, get another one. Take a clean, damp cotton rag and a dry one and wipe and dry the island around the tub. Rinse and wring out your rag again and then do the same thing to the inside, wiping and drying your way out of the tub.

7.   Tub (full clean):

   a.   Put your rug down in front of the tub and if it's a Jacuzzi type of tub, spray Tilex in all the jets and filters. Let them soak for about ten minutes and then thoroughly rinse them out. If there is a spray nozzle, use that; if not, fill a bucket up and rinse it that way. Rinse the tub thoroughly.

   b.   If the tub has an island around it and there are knick-knacks, dust the knick-knacks and any pictures with a clean, dry microfiber cloth. Then, look at the surface around the tub and see how dirty it is. Most likely, it will be dirty, so use the Soft Scrub on a clean, wet rag and wash it. Then, rinse with another clean, wet rag and dry it, making sure you get all of the hair, spray, etc., off the surface. Again, you might have to go over it a couple of times. Use your dry hand to check to see if it's clean or not.

   c.   Once that is all done, put some Soft Scrub in the tub and then, with a wet cotton or microfiber rag, scrub the tub and hardware. If it's brass, don't use Soft Scrub – instead, try to clean it instead with a wet rag and then with a dry rag (the microfiber rags are great for this). Make sure you remove all the soap scum. Rinse and repeat if necessary.

   d.   Dry the tub with cotton rags until you have gotten all of the water and Soft Scrub off. Shine the hardware and then use your dry hand to run over everything to see if you've got it completely clean.

8. Mirrors:

   a.   Spray your diluted Windex on the mirror, using enough to get off the toothpaste, etc. You might have to let it soak or go over the tough spots a couple of times. Spray the entire mirror and wipe off with your clean cotton towel.

   b.   Then, get a dry section of the rag and spray just a very light amount, a section at a time. This will take the smears off.

   c.   If it is still smeared and/or it has lint on it, use the special microfiber E cloth rag or soft t-shirt to polish it.

   d.   Bend down and look at the mirror from different angles to see if you missed anything. Remember, do not clean glass or mirrors with light shining directly on them – they will keep smearing!

9. Sinks:

   a.   Fill soap dispensers as needed. Don't do this each week; fill them only when they get about half empty.

   b.   Check to see if the tissues need to be replaced as well.

   c.   Take your gloves off and wash your hands with soap. Grab the toothbrushes and wash them by running them under water and removing the toothpaste. Rinse them thoroughly and dry them. Do the same for electric toothbrushes. If rubbing alcohol is available, pour some over the bristles, wait for a few seconds, and then thoroughly rinse them. Wrap them up in some tissues and set them aside where they will not get dirty.

d. Now, start by quickly wiping off any of the knick-knacks on the counter with a damp cotton rag and dry with another cotton rag. This includes soap dispensers, toothbrush holders, cups, and so on. Dry and polish each item. Hold it up to the light to see if there are any smears. If possible, move the items to one side of the sink so that you can clean the other. If you're not able to do this, then get a towel and set the items on the tub or somewhere out of the way so they don't get broken.

e. Wet a cotton rag and wash the walls and/or backsplash around the sink and around and under all the towel racks in the bathroom, wringing out your rag as needed. If the backsplash has a shiny finish, you will have to dry it to prevent streaks.

f. Now, use a little bit of Soft Scrub on a wet cotton rag. Scrub the sink, counter, and hardware with Soft Scrub. Again, if the hardware is brass, just try to clean it first with a wet rag and then with a dry rag – don't use Soft Scrub. Rinse, dry and shine. Pay attention to corners, edges, and behind and under faucets, etc. If the counter is stained, you can use Bar Keeper's Friend to get the tough stains off. Be careful though, and make sure these products are safe to use on the surface.

g. If there are two sinks in the bathroom, you'll need to do the same to the other.

h. When finished, check the mirror again to see if you got it dirty when you were cleaning the sink and counter. If you did, of course, clean it off.

i. Put the knick-knacks and toothbrushes back where they belong.

j. Wet a rag and wash the outside of all the cabinets in the bathroom, paying special attention to the handles and around the handles.

10. Bathroom towels and rugs:

a. Once the bathrooms are clean, fold and hang up the clean towels that match the bathroom. Try to put out two of everything: two wash rags, towels, and face towels. Leave a bath rug/towel to place on the floor in front of the shower or tub for people to use when they get out to dry their feet and to keep the floor dry. Some people have special rugs for this. If they do, of course, use those. Also, put the clean rugs down after the floor has been washed.

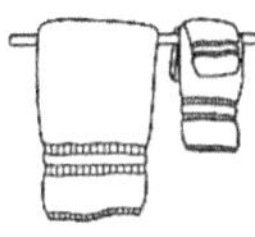

b.   Note: if they use a bath towel/rug to wipe their feet after the shower or bath, fold it neatly and lay it over the tub or shower door.

Changing Linens:

1.   Take the clean sheets and start with the fitted sheet. Pull it tightly over all four corners and tuck it in on the sides.

2.   Next, take the flat sheet and lay it on the bed with the tag side showing up. The top of the sheet is the part that has some sort of design or raised pattern on it. Pull that up to the top of the bed, making sure all sides are even. Don't let one side be longer than the other: It looks bad and will sometimes show below the bedspread.

3.   Now, take the blanket – not the bedspread – and lay it over the flat sheet, leaving it about seven inches from the top of the bed. Make sure all sides are exactly even.

4.   Take the top section of the flat sheet and fold it over about six inches until it covers the top six inches of the blanket.

5.   Get the bedspread. All spreads are different, and there are so many different ways to finish the bed, so I am just going to tell you how to deal with one type. Take the straight edge of the spread and put it at the top. Normally, the bottom will be curved in some way, but not always. If it's not, you will have to play with it to see how it fits (take a picture of it before you take it apart). Once you have the spread to the top of the mattress and both sides are even, fold it down about two feet if you have enough. You are trying to fold the top part of the spread over the pillows. Now tuck the bedspread over and under the pillows.

6.   Display the decorative pillows on the bed the best you can. If you are not the most creative person on your team, call in the one who is to help you. The client can tell or show you the next time if you could not arrange them the way they like it.

Cleaning Blinds:

1. If the client has blinds all over the house, I would just save them for when you do extras, such as when they are out of town or when they pay you to come and do extras.

2. If they only have a few blinds, then I would take care of them every couple of weeks, especially if they are in the bathrooms – but clean them before you clean the bathroom or dust the house.

3. Use a bucket of Murphy Oil Soap, mixed with water, and a cotton rag. Start by wiping off the windowsill. Then, wipe only the top of each slat. Don't forget to pay attention to the side edges, around the strings that hold the blind together, as well as the hardware for opening and closing the blinds. Unless you are doing a major cleaning, all you need to do is the top part of each blind, not underneath it. Remember to dry your opposite hand so that when you touch the clean section, you will not get it dirty. Also, remember that when you're ready to wring out your rag, slightly turn up the last slat you've cleaned so you can remember where you left off.

Dusting:

1. Make a bucket of Murphy Oil Soap mixed with water. Hang a bottle of Windex over the bucket (but remember – be careful not to let the bottle slide to the end of the bucket because when you pick up the bucket, it could tip over and spill water all over the floor), grab a few microfiber rags, one for the water and the other two for your pocket, and a dry cotton rag for glass tables. (Shake all of your rags outside before you start.)

2. Start at one corner of the room and work your way around the perimeter. Then make your way into the center of the room, dusting every item. Continue dusting this way from the outer wall of the perimeter to the middle of the room. Do this at every house every time so you do not miss anything. For a regular weekly cleaning, you do not have to do everything each week. Try to have the same person dust each week because they will remember what they skipped the week before.

3.   If you are in a hurry, you can skip bookshelves in living rooms or guest rooms that have not been used (or you could skip the entire room, for that matter). Don't skip these things for more than a week or so because the client will notice. You are not trying to deceive the client, you simply cannot do everything each week.

4.   Use a dry microfiber cloth quickly on legs of furniture, tops of picture frames, and knick-knacks. When dusting pictures, just dust the glass, top of frame, and any protruding ledges or lips. There is no need to wash the glass every time—save this for when you do extras. Knick-knacks just need a quick dusting, but if you see that something is smeared, then give it a polish.

5.   Wring out your wet microfiber rag thoroughly and wipe the top of a piece of furniture and any protruding ledges that catch dust. Every few weeks, dust the entire piece. If the piece of furniture is a dresser or something people get into often, wash the entire piece each time to get all the fingerprints off. You will just have to decide what needs extra attention as you go. Note if the rooms are very dusty, each week you may have to dust the sides, legs, etc.

6.   Don't forget to wash and/or polish the light switches.

7.   If there are bookshelves, use a clean, dry microfiber rag on the knick-knacks and shelves.

8.   Be careful; if the microfiber rag gets too much dust on it, you will just be moving the dirt around. Keep changing the rags when needed. You can also use the special mirror polishing rag to polish glass items if you like.

9.   If you come across leather furniture that needs to be cleaned, use a wet cotton rag to wash it, not a microfiber rag.

Scrubbing Floors:

1.   Make a bucket of Murphy Oil Soap mixed with water and get a couple of cotton rags to wash with. Murphy Oil Soap can be used on most any floor, including marble; however, on marble and shiny surfaces, you will need to wring your rag out a little tighter so that it does not leave water spots behind – or dry as you go. Feel free to use something like Pine-Sol for ceramic floors if you like. However, use very little of

this product as it leaves a residue and can make the floor sticky. Put your knee pads on, go to the top floor, and start cleaning the bathroom and bedroom floors. After those, clean the hall and wood around the steps.

2. Wring your rag out often and leave enough water on the rag to cut through the dirt – but not so much that it takes longer than sixty seconds to dry.

3. Put a dry microfiber rag in the opposite hand to the one you're using to wash the floors and dust the baseboards as you go. There is no need to do all baseboards in the house each time, except for those in bathrooms. Most of the time, these can be dry dusted. Always dust the wood baseboards on steps each cleaning; they get dirty fast. As for the rest of the baseboards, do all in one room one week and all in another room the next week; that way in about a month of weekly cleanings, you will have dusted all the baseboards in the house that are around hard floors. The others should be done when doing extras. Wash the floor going from right to left and only do as much as you can reach in each section.

4. Use things like edges of baseboards or the edge of a doorway to mark the section you are working on so that you know what you have done and what you have not done. Always overlap as you go to be sure not to miss anything.

5. If you are right-handed, keep your bucket on the right side of you at all times, and if you are left-handed, keep it on your left side.

6. Keep sliding the bucket with you to save having to get up and wring the rag out; otherwise, you will be wasting a lot of time and doing it that way is very hard on your body, especially the knees.

7. Keep changing your water and rags as needed. Make sure you wash every square inch of the floor, paying attention to the corners. You can put the rugs back down on the floor as you go or when you are done – but never put the rug back on a still-wet floor. Be sure to wipe up any dust that may have fallen on the floor from the rug.

8. Once the second floor is done, move on to the basement, if there is one and you are supposed to clean it. Clean the first floor last.

Cleaning the Kitchen:

1. Sink:

    a. Spray some Tilex Mold and Mildew Remover around the perimeter of the drain and in the sink if needed (be sure you can use Tilex on that particular finish) and let it soak. This will take off stains such as those caused by coffee that have formed around the drain and in the sink.

    b. While that is soaking, if there is a window above the kitchen sink, clean it inside and out, if possible. Feel free to use Windex and a cotton rag to dry, or use clean dishwater and a cotton rag to wash and then dry with a dry cotton rag. Finish the window by sweeping the magic e-cloth rag over the glass to get off all the lint and take out any smears that were missed.

    c. Now, rinse away the Tilex.

    d. Use Soft Scrub and a cotton rag to scrub the sink. If the sink is stained, and the Soft Scrub is not cutting it, use Barkeeper's Friend. With both, use a cotton rag to wash, rinse, and then dry. Fill the sink up with water and use a little Dawn detergent in it.

2. Refrigerator:

    a. If you are getting paid to clean inside the refrigerator, wet a cotton rag and start on the top shelf, wiping and drying as you go.

    b. Straighten things up and watch for dates that are expired and if they have, toss the item.

    c. Neatly put things back, from large in the back to small in the front, all facing forward.

    d. Go through the entire refrigerator this way, including the drawers. (You could just wipe the outside of the drawers each week and save the inside part for a day when there is time for cleaning those areas you usually can't get to. For example, the family is on vacation and the house doesn't need as much attention as usual – you can use that time to get to those areas.) If you are cleaning the fridge weekly, it should not take you very much time after the initial major cleaning of the refrigerator. Remember, it's important to use a dry cotton towel when drying off the shelves; otherwise, the moisture from the fridge will make it smear.

3. Other Appliances:

a. Using a wet cotton rag, wash the outside and inside of the microwave and then dry and polish it. If there are tough stains, spray some Windex directly on the stain and let soak for a few minutes before wiping them off.

b. Wash, dry, and shine the outside of any other appliance.

c. For stainless steel appliances such as a refrigerator, use a clean, damp cotton rag with a little Soft Scrub and wash the appliance down, going with the grain and doing sections at a time. Once you have washed the first section, use another clean, dry cotton rag and dry it off. Move to the next section and repeat. If the client has been using the stainless steel product that the manufacture recommends, then you will have to go over the appliance many times to get that product off. Don't use the stainless steel product yourself when cleaning.

d. Pay attention to the edges of the appliance; for example, if it's a refrigerator, open the door and clean the inner and outer lip around the door.

e. Once you have removed all of the greasy fingerprints, etc., use another clean, damp cotton rag and wash and dry the refrigerator again until all the Soft Scrub is off. Then use the Krystal Klear magic rag…

… by wetting it and wringing it out as tightly as you can, going over the appliance in the direction of the grain. If you do not have the magic rag, get a clean microfiber rag wet with just water, wring it out tightly, and wipe off smears, going with the grain.

f. Don't forget to clean the toaster, toaster oven, warming drawer, etc.

4. Cabinets & Counters:

a. Use your damp cotton rag to start washing the outside of the cabinets. Start at the top and work your way down, paying attention to the handles and around the handles.

b. Use a damp cotton rag and wash, dry, and polish any knick-knacks, paper towel holders, napkin holders, etc. on the counters.

c. When working on the backsplash, wring out your clean rag and wash and dry the backsplash and light switches.

d. Wash and dry the counters, working on sections at a time so that you can place the clean items back where they belong (on the clean counter). For tough spots, you can use Soft Scrub (it is okay for most counters, but make sure before you use it). If there are different levels of counter, one higher than the other, clean the top portion first. Try not to wipe the crumbs onto the floor; it has already been swept.

e. Remember to keep your water and rags clean as you go (I know I repeat this, but it's important! If you don't do this, things don't get clean, and it takes three times as long to do).

5. Finishing the Kitchen:

a. To finish, get a clean, damp rag and do one more wipe and dry over the counter, working around the knick-knacks to get any crumbs, drips, etc. that were left behind.

b. Reclean the kitchen sink. Re-scour it, rinse, dry, and polish.

c. Resweep the kitchen floor.

Cleaning the Laundry Room:

1. Use a cotton rag to wash the appliances off, including inside the washer door and around the soap dispenser, and then dry and shine.

2. Get another clean rag and wet it to wash off the fronts of the cabinets and all the counters, plus any knick-knacks.

3. If there was laundry left by the client, and if there is time, fold and stack it neatly in a corner.

Finishing Touches and Final Checks:

1. Re-scrub the kitchen floor and pathways throughout the first floor one more time.

2. Tidy the powder room. Spot-clean the toilet you have been using for

the day and fold the toilet paper. Check the floor in front of the toilet for drips.

3. Have the lead person do the last walk-through of the house, making sure everything is put back and in order, furniture is centered and placed correctly, the pictures straight on the walls, beds made perfectly, pillows fluffed and positioned in the perfect places, candles straight, bathroom rugs down, clean towels out, toilet paper folded, etc.

4. Using the carpet sweeper, start sweeping the second-floor carpet and rugs, beginning at the far end of the room and working your way back out the door, trying to make the sweeper lines as neat as you can. Scan the room once more then turn off the lights.

5. If the room has rugs with fringes, use a hair pick to neatly comb out the fringes, getting all of the tangles out so that they are all going in the same direction. Have a damp rag with you to wipe up any mess you make when combing.

6. Do this to each room, leaving the hall for last.

7. Once everything is in order and the lights are off upstairs, vacuum the carpet on the stairs. Then go and do the same to the rest of the house, but doing it in such a way that you are heading out the door, if possible. For example, if your exit door is through the laundry room area, do that room last so that no one messes up what you have done or walks on the carpet you have just vacuumed.

8. Scour the sink and rinse it out. Wash your hands and then dry and polish the sink.

9. Watch for any water spots left on the floor and wipe them up if there are.

10. Do one more, quick scan of the house, making sure you have all of your supplies, everything is in perfect order, and all doors are locked, lights off, etc.

11. Leave the house, turning on the alarm if required.

Quick cleaning tips to use only when needed:

- Dusting: You can just do the tops of things and skip the unused rooms.

- Showers: You can clean the glass, shine the fixtures, and wash the floor.

- Bathrooms: You can just wash and dry off sinks and counters in some bathrooms if they are not very dirty.

- Floors: You can use a dust mop over wood floors, but always wash hallways during each cleaning.

- Cabinets: You can wash around the handles and spot-clean the rest.

- Blinds: You can shut these and quickly wipe down the slats.

- Refrigerator: You can skip it when you don't have enough time.

CHAPTER 10

CLEANING TIPS AND REFERENCE GUIDE

As the name implies, this book has been all about ATTENTION TO DETAIL. As stated earlier, the cleaning system and tips included in this book work as well for the 20,000 square foot home as they do in a quaint bed and breakfast on the beach or any hotel.

Cleaning a luxury home—or any home, for that matter—requires more than just attention to detail. It demands significant time and effort, and rushing through the job or taking shortcuts is not an option. However, if you clean smartly and efficiently, you can complete each task correctly the first time, ultimately saving you energy and time.

In my early years cleaning homes, I quickly learned there is a right way and a wrong way to do each step of the process – and was able to implement time-saving techniques in my cleaning routine. This chapter pulls together some of these techniques and tips to help you and your cleaning team do a detailed and amazing job – and do it in the most efficient way possible. Some of the tips below have already been written in other chapters, but this section is designed to give you a quick reference guide – please use it that way!

Products the Client Pays For:

- **Tilex® Mold and Mildew** is used to remove mold, mildew and other such tough stains in kitchen sinks, bathrooms or laundry areas. It has a strong smell, so be sure to use it in a well ventilated area. Always carry it in a bucket and place a rag over it to prevent any drips. Drips or spills of this product can stain or damage any surface if you are not careful.

- **SoftScrub®** (without bleach) is an all-purpose general cleanser which works well for cleaning sinks, counters, tubs, showers, scuffs on painted doors and baseboards, etc.

- **Toilet Cleaner** (without bleach) is used for the obvious – to clean the toilet bowl. Lysol® Toilet Cleaner is what I normally used.

- **Windex® Glass Cleaner** used for windows, glass table tops, mirrors and other glass surfaces. Each bottle of window cleaner should be diluted with two parts water to one part Windex. If the home has a water softener, use bottled water instead. This would result in two bottles of glass cleaner. Be sure to save empty bottles for this purpose.

- **Murphy Oil Soap Original** is a great general purpose, light-smelling cleaning product that cleans most hard surfaces, blinds, woodwork, floors, door knobs and more. Note that if the water is looking dirty, it needs to be changed. Remember, less is more for this product!

- **Dawn Dishwashing Liquid** is good to use for dishes and those home décor items that are washed by hand. It can also be used for cleaning mirrors and windows. Remember, less is more for this product.

- **PineSol®** can be used instead of Murphy Oil Soap to clean ceramic or vinyl floors. Never use it on wood floors, though.

- **Bar Keepers Friend®** does a great job on stainless steel or porcelain sinks, stove tops and other such surfaces. Use only the powdered cleaner, not the soft cleanser. 

- **Brass Cleaner** is for cleaning brass items in the home. Wright's® and Brasso are both good products to use, and come in a cream or liquid form.

- **Wright's® Silver Cream** is used to clean the good silver, trays, bowls, and other silver serving pieces. 

- **Oven Cleaner** products on the market now are fume-free; check to make sure the oven can be cleaned with a particular product. Most ovens are self-cleaning, and should **not** be cleaned with oven cleaner as it can damage the oven interior. Oven cleaner does a great job on oven racks. Be sure to clean the racks outside the home if possible for ventilation. 

- **Baking Soda** is used to control strong odors in the refrigerator and freezer. Put one in each refrigerator and freezer, and be sure to change it every six months.

- **Mr. Clean® Magic Erasers** helps remove those tough marks on walls and painted baseboards. Do a spot test first because this can scratch the paint.

- **Trash Bags** in 5, 13 and 30 gallon capacity – get a name brand like Glad® or Hefty® that you know is strong.

- **Marblelife Maxout Grout Cleaner** works well for cleaning all grout, including showers and bath tile and ceramic or other tile floors.

- **Rubbing alcohol** is especially good to use in the home during cold and flu season, or when someone has been sick. Wipe door knobs and other handles off with alcohol to help kill germs. Do a test spot first because alcohol can damage some finishes. Do not use on brass.

Products & Supplies that you provide:

- **Riccar SupraLife Premium R10P** with a lifetime belt and 20-foot cord. Not only is this a light-weight vacuum and easy to carry back and forth, but it has two settings. One is for vacuuming expensive and more fragile carpets or rugs such as an Oriental rug that requires careful, light vacuuming. The second setting is for the more durable carpets.

- **Sanitaire SC3683 Mighty Mite Canister** which you can find on Sanitaire or Amazon. I recommend also buying the HEPA #253 filter to put on the back of the sweeper. This unit has amazing suction and attachments that work well for vacuuming curtains, sofas, and other pieces of furniture. It also has a great attachment for sweeping hard floors. You could also use the Eureka brand; they have the same type of sweepers. Be careful to not let the cord rub against the corners of baseboards, doors, wall edges, and so on as it will leave a mark.

- **Spider web wand,** also called a cobweb duster. These generally have a polyfiber head and long pole that extends to clean ceilings and other hard-to-reach areas. Having a 12-foot pole will help you reach those really high ceilings.

- **Microfiber rags** in various sizes and thickness are a must-have. They are lint-free, pick up dust like a magnet, and can be easily washed. **You need at least 20**. Microfiber rags should be washed only with other microfiber rags in lukewarm water and a small amount of good detergent, generally 1/4 the amount recommended on the container. If the rags are very dirty, use a little more soap. Wash and rinse, then do a second rinse (with cold water) in the washing machine. Do not put microfiber rags in the clothes dryer. Instead, let them air-dry on a rack. Keep these rags in a separate bag from the cotton rags.

- **E-Cloth Dusting Cloth®** (Magic Rag) is a square cloth for dusting that is washable and can be used over and over. It is ideal for putting the finishing touches on that just-cleaned mirror or for wiping down the glass in framed pictures. These can be washed with the microfiber rags.

- **Krystal Clear** microfiber cleaning cloths work great for quick-cleaning of stainless steel and glass household items that just need a touch-up.

- **White cotton bar towels** are great for cleaning kitchens, laundry rooms and bathrooms, floors, etc. You need at least 40 to start. Wash them in hot water using the recommended amount of detergent shown on the bottle or box of a good laundry detergent. Add a half cup of bleach to the bleach dispenser. Never pour bleach directly onto the clothes or rags in the washer.

  You will do a second cold water rinse, this time adding a cup of distilled white vinegar to the rinse water. The vinegar cuts down on the amount of lint left on the rag and also increases absorption. Put the towels in the dryer and run it until they are dry. Clean the lint filter and dry them for another 10 minutes to remove more lint. It's also a good idea to vigorously shake each rag outside to be sure as much lint as possible has been removed.

  Do not use fabric softener when washing any cleaning rags or towels!

- **Rubber gloves** to protect hands from being in water and cleaning solutions all day. Gloves also protect from germs, exposure to harsh chemicals and so on.

- **Lint brush** is used to get excess animal fur or hair from carpets, floors and furniture.

- **Large rug** to protect floors from the splashed products when cleaning the bathrooms, kitchens, silver and so on.

- **Toothbrush** for cleaning tight spaces like behind a bathroom faucet, around the toilet hardware, etc.

- **2 or 3 old large towels** which can be used to wipe spills, or in place of the large rug listed above.

- **Old, soft T-shirts** work well in putting the final touch on glass, and easily remove smears and lint from a cotton cleaning rag. These can be washed along with the microfiber rags.

- **Scrub buckets, 14 quart** are needed and it's a good idea to have one bucket for each person cleaning with you on any day.

- **Knee pads** for each of your workers. This helps protect knees when cleaning hard floors or kneeling to clean toilets, bathtubs, etc. Note: don't use knee pads with rubber; they will scuff the floors.

- **Nail polish remover** is a good tool to use to remove sticky glue and bits of price tags you couldn't peel off that were on mirrors, the glass in a picture frame, cups, dishes or glass cookware, and so on.

Floors and carpets …

- If you clean a home every other week, suggest to the client that all rugs, along with hardwood, tile or vinyl floors be swept or vacuumed the week you're not there to clean. This will help reduce the amount of dust that gets onto the furniture, countertops, plants and other household décor – and will make a huge difference in how the house looks in-between cleanings. It may even make them realize they need you every week!

- Put the soft side of Velcro strips around the floor cleaning attachments (canister sweeper attachments). You can also put it on the bottom edge of the carpet sweeper.

- Be sure not to let sweeper cords rub against baseboards, doors, wall edges, and so on, as they will leave a mark.

- Vacuum floors and rugs in each room first before you start to clean the bathrooms, dust furniture or scrub floors.

- Use the tile sweeper attachment to clean corners and along the edges of a wall in rooms that have wall to wall carpeting.

- Take throw rugs outside and shake them vigorously to remove all excess dirt and dust before vacuuming. Never shake them inside the home! Smaller rugs should be washed every other week or weekly if they get dirty quickly.

- If a section of the carpet is discolored – perhaps something was spilled on it like bleach – try using a permanent marker to match and fill in the color. Craft stores are a good place to find a wide selection of marker colors – it shouldn't be too hard to find one that matches.

- Never use a broom to sweep inside – use a canister sweeper. Brooms do nothing but move the dust and dirt around – and make the cleaning job that much harder.

- Never use a mop to clean a floor – it will not do a good job and won't get the dirt and dust from the edges or out of the corners. Instead, always scrub floors on your hands and knees using knee pads for protection. You will get the floor so much cleaner and can get in the corners and edges better with your hands and fingers than you can with a mop. Be sure to press hard enough to remove the dirt but not so hard that your hand and arm hurt after ten minutes.

- Murphy Oil Soap works well for cleaning most tile or wood floors. Use just a teaspoon of the soap in a bucket with a gallon of water. If the floor is very dirty, the rag should be wet enough to cut through the dirt. Otherwise, use a little less water on the rag. Again, cleaning on hands and knees not only does a better job, but you are protecting the floor against damage from too much water.

- Be careful how much product you use. Less is more with cleaning products; the more you use, the more you will have to remove. Too much

   TIM ROSSHIRT

will also attract dirt. For example, too much Murphy's Oil Soap on the floor can cause the floor to streak and attract dirt from shoes, etc.

- Wringing excess water out of the rag helps prevent leaving streaks on marble flooring.

- When scrubbing the floor, keep a dry microfiber rag under the hand you are not scrubbing with – this prevents hand prints on the wet floor and also takes a little pressure off your arm.

- A pencil eraser can be used to remove scuff marks on some floors.

- Don't forget outside entrances and porches, patios or decks. These areas need to be kept clean. For example, the front porch should be swept clean with a broom, and any outside rugs should be shaken to remove dirt, and vacuumed or washed. This prevents dirt from getting tracked back inside the house. Keep all walkways and stairs leading into the home or garage clean, and free of dust and dirt. Placing an outside rug or mat in front of the door for people to wipe their feet on before coming into the house can help a lot.

- Take care of your sweepers and vacuums. Never yank the sweeper cords out; remove them by grabbing the plug end of the sweeper that is plugged into the wall. Replace bags in all sweepers and vacuums when they need to be, and keep them well-maintained so they work properly for you. I recommend replacing the bags when they are no more than half-full or sooner. Note: brush strips on the carpet vacuums wear down eventually and will need to be replaced.

In the kitchen, bathrooms and laundry …

- Remove and throw away ice from the ice bin at least every two weeks (once a week is best, though) to keep it fresh. Make sure to clean and thoroughly dry the ice bin before putting it back in the freezer.

- Keep a fresh box of baking soda in the refrigerator and freezer to help remove odors. Remove the old box and put a new box in every 3 to 6 months. Be sure and write the date on the box – this makes it easy to remember when it's time to replace. Don't forget the refrigerators or freezers in the basement or garage.

- When washing dishes by hand, use Dawn® dishwashing liquid. Start with a half teaspoon or less. When using the dishwasher, Cascade® with Dawn (or any other dishwasher detergent that has Dawn in it) is going to do the job – and will make the dishes come out looking like new!

- Jet-Dry® is another great product to use in the dishwasher and will help prevent water spots – most dishwashers have a built-in dispenser for this. If you're not sure where it is, check the user manual.

- Be careful how you load the dishwasher. Do not overload it, and make sure no dishes are blocking the vents or jets – that prevents water from reaching all the dishes. Also check to make sure the jets can move freely before you run the dishwasher.

- Always pre-spot clothes and other laundry items with Shout® or a similar liquid stain remover before washing them. I think Shout is the best I've used so far.

- Use ½ cup chlorine bleach in the washer to keep white clothes, towels, and such at their whitest. Never pour directly on the clothes; use the bleach dispenser.

- Clean and sanitize waste baskets and trash cans with bleach or Tilex to kill germs and strong smells.

- To clean plastic cutting boards, spray Tilex Mildew on, then let soak for 10 minutes. After that, thoroughly wash with Soft Scrub. If possible, then put in the dishwasher to remove all bleach.

- In addition to using Tilex® Mold and Mildew to remove mold and mildew in the tub and shower, it removes coffee and other stains in the sink and drain. Spray the cleaner around the stains that build up around the drain, let it sit for five minutes and then rinse.

- To remove stains from grout in the tile floors or other tiled-areas in the home, use Marblelife Maxout Grout Cleaner. It does a great job.

- If your rubber gloves get wet inside, turn them inside out after removing and let dry. To prepare for proper use, flip to the correct side, then blow air into them, and presto!

- Wash cotton rags in hot water with laundry soap at ½ cup of bleach. Let run through entire cycle, then turn back on for another rinse and add ½ cup – 1 cup of distilled vinegar to the rinse water. This will help reduce the lint and help rags absorb more water. When finished drying your rags, clean lint trap and then turn the dryer back on for about 10 more minutes. This will help reduce the amount of lint on your rags.

- Wash microfiber rags by themselves; never put cotton rags with them. Wash on warm with less than ¼ of the recommended amount of detergent from the container. If the rags are very dirty, use a little more. Wash and rinse them, then do a second rinse with cold water. Hang these rags to dry; never put in the dryer.

- Always shake all of your rags outside before using them. This will help keep the lint out of the house and make your job easier.

- After washing client towels, turn the washer on for another rinse and add ½-1 cup of distilled vinegar to the rinse water. This will help their towels absorb water faster.

Throughout the home …

- If there is melted candle wax on carpeting or cloth furniture, do the following:

- Cover the wax with a brown paper bag

- Hold a warm iron over the bag until you see the wax begin to soak into the bag

- Move a clean section of the bag over the wax and repeat the steps above

- Continue to move the bag over the wax and iron until the wax is gone

- Windex Window Cleaner is used to clean windows, mirrors, glass, etc. I always diluted the glass cleaner two-to-one (two parts water to one-part Windex) with tap water. Remember, if the client has a water softener, use bottled or distilled water, not tap water, to dilute the window cleaner.

- Direct sun or heat from lights above a window or mirror can cause smears. Wait until the sun has moved and/or turn off the light before cleaning glass, windows or mirrors. This is a good tip when cleaning your car windows, too.

- Never use paper towels or newspapers to clean glass or windows. I prefer to use cotton rags; they do a much better job.

- Pet hair that remains after vacuuming can be lifted from a carpet or furniture using a damp clean microfiber rag or a lint brush. If there are multiple pets in the home – or one hairy one – you may need to use both.

- Always dust from top to bottom – if you start at the bottom and work your way up, you are simply throwing dust down to an area already cleaned – and then you get to dust again.

- Nail polish remover can be used to remove sticky residue left from a store price tag on glass items, including mirrors, dishes, coffee mugs, etc.

- If a lamp shade is new and in good condition, it can be gently vacuumed using a small, soft-brush sweeper attachment.

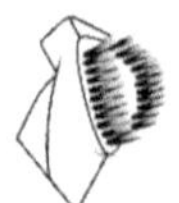

If the lamp shade is old or an antique, don't vacuum, as you risk tearing or otherwise damaging it, and having to replace the shade. A clean dry microfiber cloth can be used for dusting it instead. Start at the top of the lamp shade and gently work your way down and around, using the seam as the starting point. Be sure to dust the top and bottom edge of the shade, as well as the inside.

- When cleaning doors and baseboards, remove as much dust as possible first by using the canister sweeper attachment. This is especially important if the wood has not been cleaned in a while. Then clean with a solution of Murphy Oil Soap and water. Use a soft toothbrush to get into any grooves or corners in order to get those areas clean.

- Use a white cotton rag to clean cabinets, woodwork, cupboards, etc. If the cotton rag isn't doing the job, use a damp microfiber rag. Microfiber rags can sometimes get through the grease a little better.

- If you are using a ladder to clean areas inside the home that are otherwise too high to reach, you need to protect the floors. Get four cotton rags and securely tape a rag using Duck Tape (or some other strong tape) around each leg of the ladder. This keeps you from

TIM ROSSHIRT

scratching or scuffing floors, and also prevents dirt that may be on the ladder legs from getting on carpets, rugs or floors.

- Never clean with a sponge. They leave streaks and smears and quickly become smelly and unsanitary. Use cotton rags instead.

- I would wash baseboards and clean both sides of glass tables at least every three months, unless they have kids; then do it more often.

- Ceiling fans and lights should be cleaned at least twice a year.

General household maintenance tips …

- Check furnace filters every three months, and change them if needed; otherwise change them every six months. Changing filters regularly helps keep dust down in the home.

- Air ducts need to be professionally cleaned, and should be done every two years. This also greatly reduces how much dust is in your home.

- Dryer vents should also be cleaned every two years and a professional may be needed to get the job done right. The vent should be cleaned from the point where it is attached to the back of the clothes dryer all the way through the home to where it vents directly outside. The dryer vent hose should also be checked regularly to make sure it's attached securely to the back of the dryer so lint doesn't end up in the house. Dryer hose/vent tape can be purchased at any home improvement store if needed.

- Purchase Ortho Home Defense and spray it around the interior and exterior throughout the house. It should be applied everywhere in the home: crawlspace, attic, garage, basement and utility room. Be sure to spray around baseboards and in the corners. Not only does this prevent spiders and other insects from getting into the home, it also helps prevent spider webs from popping up and reduces your cleaning time. I normally do this twice per year.

Tips for your own home …

- It can be hard to keep up with things in your own home, especially after working five days a week cleaning other people's home. Here are some suggestions to make the home look clean, even if you know it's really not up to your standards:

- Keep everything picked up and organized in each room – the home will look cleaner than you know it is.

- Get rid of clutter and toss out what you don't need. Make three piles: what you want to keep, what you will donate, and what goes in the trash. Decide in five seconds what pile an item will go into, and put it there. Do not rethink your decision – stick with your instinct. Take what should be tossed to the trash can, place what is to be donated into a box and put that in your car, and put what you are keeping in its proper place. Now you are done!

- If your home needs to be cleaned and organized, organize one day and clean another. This will be less stressful and you are not rushing to get more done in a day than you can possibly do.

These cleaning tips are a summary of the basic housecleaning steps that need **your attention to detail** in every client's home. Following the full step-by-step system explained thoroughly in the major and general cleaning chapters of this book can be your step-by-step guide to a successful and lucrative cleaning business.

CHAPTER 11

IN CLOSING

Thank you for taking the time to read this book. I hope it has strengthened your determination to have a successful cleaning business and helps you become the best cleaning professional in your city. The tips contained within this book are tested and true – and can guide you in providing a meticulous, detailed cleaning every step of the way. You can do this; just believe that you can!

If you believe you can or believe you can't, both are true for you.

- Henry Ford

I want to share with you another passion of mine – the Rosshirt Water for Africa Foundation which I started in 2009 to help provide sanitary and accessible water to thousands of people in Zimbabwe. To date, the foundation and our amazing donors have drilled and provided ongoing maintenance for 13 wells in different regions of this impoverished country. These wells provide safe water to over 80,000 people each day!

Here is my abbreviated version of this journey. It started in 2006, when I met an amazing woman named Sabhera who had just moved to the U.S. from Zimbabwe. Sabhera worked at the dry-cleaning store I patronized. Since I was there every week, we quickly got to know each other. It didn't take long for Sabhera to open up and tell me more about why she left the country where she was born.

Learning that people were dying from filthy, germ-laden water was hard to comprehend – but that's all they had to drink or cook with. It was just as difficult to imagine children not being able to go to school because they had to walk miles each day to find the nearest source of water, which was most likely unclean and contaminated – and then walk the same miles to get back home lugging a heavy bucket of water. If there were no children, then usually the women in the family – young and old – went off each day to fetch water.

I couldn't imagine the other horrific conditions people had to deal with in that country –no sanitation systems, people starving from having very little food, an extreme lack of medical care, a corrupt government and so much more devastation. The more Sabhera told me, the more I wanted to help.

Determined to do something, I reached out to my family, friends and clients, asking for donations so we could help. Within one month, I raised $6,000 which was used to buy two semi-truck loads of food and grain that we purchased from the Zimbabwe government. Sabhera was so excited and arranged for her brother, who still lived in Zimbabwe, to help me get things done!

I made my first trip to Zimbabwe later that year to oversee the food distribution which helped hundreds of families. I also passed out toothpaste and toothbrushes, special items for the children, school supplies and anything else I could get donated.

   TIM ROSSHIRT

What I saw during my week in Zimbabwe was more than the intolerable living conditions – I realized that the biggest problem facing these people was not having clean and sanitary drinking water every day. I quickly realized that the rate of water-related incidences of dysentery and cholera, even death, was even higher than I was told.

It was a little boy who wasn't any older than four begging me for the bottle of water I held in my hands that inspired me. He didn't ask for food or money – all he wanted was water to drink.

I realized that helping the people of Zimbabwe have safe and accessible drinking water was the true focus of the Rosshirt Water for Africa Foundation, and the beginning of our real journey. This ongoing journey is to find sources of water where we can build and maintain clean, safe wells for the villages of this under-developed country.

That was the start of the Rosshirt Water for Africa Foundation. As we continue our mission to quench the thirst of these incredible people, we are currently raising funds to build and maintain more wells, as well as to repair existing wells that have fallen into disrepair due to a lack of care. *We continue to bring renewed hope to the thousands of people we help every day.*

The success of the Rosshirt Water For Africa Foundation would not have been so high if it wasn't for the strong relationship I had with many of my clients. A large number of them have been major donors to the foundation from the start and I cannot thank them enough. This is another example of how going above and beyond for your clients pays off! ☺

You can read more about what we have accomplished over the years online at http://rosshirtwaterforafricafoundation.com/about-us/the-rwfa-story/ and if you can help with a donation, your support is gratefully appreciated.

www.ingramcontent.com/pod-product-compliance
Lightning Source LLC
Chambersburg PA
CBHW040146160726
48006CB00014B/1634